DEFEND/
DEFUND

DEFEND/
DEFUND

A Visual History of Organizing against the Police

Interference Archive
Edited by Brooke Darrah Shuman, Jen Hoyer, and Josh MacPhee

COMMON
NOTIONS

Philadelphia, PA
Brooklyn, NY

Defend / Defund: A Visual History of Organizing against the Police
By Interference Archive, edited by Brooke Darrah Shuman, Jen Hoyer, and
Josh MacPhee

ISBN: 978-1-942173-88-5 | eBook ISBN: 978-1-945335-01-3
Library of Congress Number: 2023945060
10 9 8 7 6 5 4 3 2 1

Common Notions
c/o Interference Archive
314 7th St.
Brooklyn, NY 11215

Common Notions
c/o Making Worlds Bookstore
210 S. 45th St.
Philadelphia, PA 19104

Discounted bulk quantities of our books are available for organizing,
educational, or fundraising purposes. Please contact Common Notions at the
address above for more information.

Cover design by Josh MacPhee
Layout design and typesetting by Partner & Partners
partnerandpartners.com

Printed by union labor in Canada on acid-free paper

This project was organized and researched by Brooke Darrah Shuman, Jen Hoyer, and Josh MacPhee, with research help from Shiva Addanki, Maggie Schriener, and Greg Mihalko. This project draws on the collection of Interference Archive and, as such, is not comprehensive; we hope it will inspire you to ask questions, look for other materials, and explore this history in your own communities.

We are grateful to Mariame Kaba and Andrea Ritchie for their editorial advice. Thank you to Dennis Flores, Mariame Kaba, Joshua Myers, Dread Scott, Jawanza Williams, Cheryl Rivera, Micah Bazant, Annie Tan, and Bianca Cunningham for sharing their knowledge and experience.

Interference Archive is grateful to the incredible support of its volunteers and its donor community, who invest their time and money in believing that another archive is possible.

TABLE OF
CONTENTS

INTRODUCTION

The history of policing in the United States is inextricably tied to the control and punishment of communities of color, in particular Black communities. Since colonial settlers arrived in the Americas, and throughout the nearly 250 years of chattel slavery, Black, Latinx, Asian, and Indigenous communities formed autonomous self-defense groups to protect themselves from the violence of white supremacy. In the 1960s and 1970s, groups like the Black Panther Party for Self-Defense and the Young Lords formalized these activities, and in the 1980s and 1990s, organizations like CopWatch and the Stolen Lives Project began recording, monitoring, and reporting on police misconduct and memorializing victims of police violence that the press and the courts ignored. Families have publicly mourned the death of loved ones at the hands of the police; communities have rioted to take back their streets in the face of injustice. The modern Defund movement, rooted in abolition philosophy and popularized by the Movement for Black Lives after the 2020 murders of George Floyd, Breonna Taylor, and Tony McDade, demands economic justice by allocating funds from police budgets to underfunded schools, hospitals, and public housing as well as reparations for victims of police violence. This movement imagines alternatives to police, that address harm while being accountable to the people.

The history of the movement to resist police violence and defund the police is part of a larger struggle to end violence against Black lives, and this work necessarily overlaps with resistance to the larger carceral system in America, from the school-to-prison pipeline to mass incarceration of Black Americans. The goal of this project is to situate today's movement to defund the police within this long history of imagining other forms of community safety and dignity, and constructing an abolitionist future. That said, incarceration in the US demands its own dedicated project, so we will touch on it but it won't be the focus here.

This is a starting point. While we have not intentionally omitted any parts of the history of communities fighting police violence, this history is so expansive that we cannot be exhaustive. The geographic scope is limited to the United States, and much of the archival material we share is from New York City. We hope you will ask questions that point to the gaps you find in this short narrative, that explore the ways this history has impacted the communities where you live, and that help this become, in turn, a resource for others to learn with and organize with.

"After Anthony was killed, they retrained police. After Eric Garner was killed, they retrained police. We don't want to hear about any more trainings—trainings don't hold police accountable, trainings don't lead to firings, trainings only give the police more money. The Mayor and NYPD's process is fake and will make no change. The only way to make change is to have other people—not the NYPD and not de Blasio—have control of the process and families like mine need to help lead that."

Iris Baez, the mother of Anthony Baez, killed by an officer with an illegal chokehold in 1994, in her 2021 testimony to City Council about police reform.

CAUTION!!

COLORED PEOPLE

OF BOSTON, ONE & ALL,

You are hereby respectfully CAUTIONED and advised, to avoid conversing with the

Watchmen and Police Officers of Boston,

For since the recent ORDER OF THE MAYOR & ALDERMEN, they are empowered to act as

KIDNAPPERS
AND
Slave Catchers,

And they have already been actually employed in KIDNAPPING, CATCHING, AND KEEPING SLAVES. Therefore, if you value your LIBERTY, and the *Welfare of the Fugitives* among you, Shun them in every possible manner, as so many *HOUNDS* on the track of the most unfortunate of your race.

Keep a Sharp Look Out for KIDNAPPERS, and have TOP EYE open.

April 24, 1851

Reprinted in 1998.

resistant strains
maximum security
democracy series

Resistant Strains, *Caution!! Colored People of Boston*, 1998 reprint of poster from 1851. This poster shows a notice created by abolitionist Thomas Parker in 1851 following the 1850 passage of the Fugitive Slave Act.

LEGACIES OF VIOLENCE

The earliest police forces in the US grew out of colonial armies and militias formed to wage war against and dispossess Indigenous people. In the early eighteenth century, slave patrols were created in slaveholding states to quell resistance and pursue enslaved people who had run away from plantations. The Fugitive Slave Acts of 1793 and 1850 gave license to law enforcement in non-slaveholding states to focus their attention on kidnapping Black people and returning them to the South (whether they were actually escaped, freed, or even born free often made little difference).

After the Civil War and the Emancipation Proclamation this oppression continued, through Reconstruction and beyond. It was notably perpetuated by armed white groups such as the Ku Klux Klan—whose membership often overlapped with local police forces—but also systematized through Jim Crow laws (in the 19th century, "Jim Crow" was a racial slur used against Black people). Other state- and city-funded law enforcement and paramilitary formations were created in the 19th century to crack down on labor organizing, quell unrest in immigrant ghettos, enforce gender binaries and sexual norms, and police people of color.

(Left) *Blue By Day White By Night, Stop Killer Cops,* button, n.d.
(Middle) *Ban the Klan,* button, n.d.
(Right) *United We Stand Anti-Klan,* button, n.d.

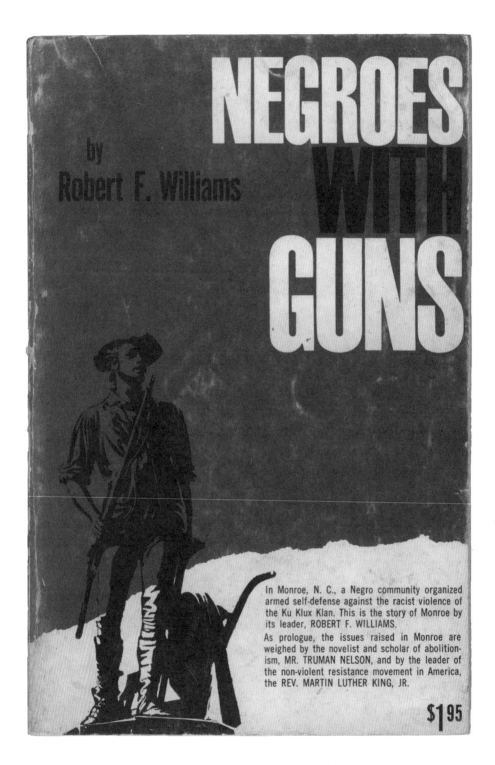

Robert F. Williams, *Negroes with Guns*, (New York, NY: Marzani & Munsell), book, 1962.

SELF-DEFENSE

One of the most influential thinkers in armed self-defense for communities of color was Robert F. Williams. Williams and his wife Mabel formed and led the chapter of the National Association for the Advancement of Colored People (NAACP) in Monroe, North Carolina in the late 1950s. The chapter fought housing and economic discrimination and worked to protect the city's Black community from both the Ku Klux Klan and the white establishment. But every one of their victories was met with increased terrorism from the KKK; when they successfully integrated the local library, the Klan staged mass rallies and sent nightly armed motorcades to terrorize the community. When they attempted to integrate the community swimming pools, the Klan created a petition signed by 6,000 residents demanding that Williams and his "Communist" members should be driven from town.

Williams's NAACP pleaded for the city to protect Black families from the escalating violence, but law enforcement did not intervene. In fact, the members of the Klan and local police forces were often one-and-the-same. It was then that Robert Williams decided to make their chapter the first fully armed branch of the NAACP. He later wrote, "when an oppressed people show a willingness to defend themselves, the enemy, who is a moral weakling and coward, is more willing to grant concessions and work for a respectable compromise." Robert Williams's book *Negroes with Guns*, and later his radio program "Radio Free Dixie"— broadcast from his exile in Cuba—inspired self-defense movements of the 1960s and 1970s from the Deacons of Defense to the Black Panther Party.

In the late 1960s, the Black Panther Party, the Young Lords Party, and I Wor Kuen all created planks in their party platforms to address policing. The Black Panthers and Young Lords established their own armed citizens' patrols. For the Panthers, item seven of their 10 Point Program states: "We want an immediate end to POLICE BRUTALITY and MURDER of Black people." This is clarified further in their later What We Believe statement: "We believe we can end police brutality in our Black community by organizing Black self-defense groups that are dedicated to defending our Black community from racist police oppression and brutality. The second Amendment of the Constitution of the United States gives us the right to bear arms. We therefore believe that all Black people should arm themselves for self-defense."

The Puerto Rican Young Lords Organization—which grew out of a street gang in Chicago in 1968—addressed police abuse through armed self-defense as one of its first organized activities, and this work continued when the group spread to New York City and became the Young Lords Party. That same year, the American Indian Movement created the AIM Patrol in Minneapolis to monitor and resist police abuse and respond to conflict in the community without violence. I Wor Kuen, formed in 1969, produced a *12 Point Program and Platform* that states, "We want to improve the living conditions of our people and are preparing to defend our communities against oppression and for revolutionary armed war against the gangsters, businessmen, politicians, and police." The Young Lords, Black Panthers, I Wor Kuen and AIM were all targeted by the FBI with extensive police violence, infiltration, and assassinations through COINTELPRO (COvert INTelligence PROgram), which had shifted its attention in 1967 from the Civil Rights Movement to these newer, more militant organizations.

(Left) *Support Indian Resistance, button,* button, 1970.
(Right) *Native American Support Network, Free Skyhorse & Mohawk: Stop All FBI Attacks,* button, 1975.

SERVE THE PEOPLE!

BLACK PANTHER PARTY
PLATFORM AND PROGRAM

1. We want freedom. We want power to determine the destiny of our Black Community.
 We believe that black people will not be free until we are able to determine our destiny.

2. We want full employment for our people.
 We believe that the federal government is responsible and obligated to give every man employment or a guaranteed income. We believe that if the white American businessmen will not give full employment, then the means of production should be taken from the businessmen and placed in the community so that the people of the community can organize and employ all of its people and give a high standard of living.

3. We want an end to the robbery by the CAPITALIST of our Black Community.

4. We want decent housing, fit for shelter of human beings.
 We believe that if the white landlords will not give decent housing to our black community, then the housing and the land should be made into cooperatives so that our community, with government aid, can build and make decent housing for its people.

5. We want education for our people that exposes the true nature of this decadent American society. We want education that teaches us our true history and our role in the present-day society.
 We believe in an educational system that will give to our people a knowledge of self. If a man does not have knowledge of himself and his position in society and the world, then he has little chance to relate to anything else.

6. We want all black men to be exempt from military service.
 We believe that Black people should not be forced to fight in the military service to defend a racist government that does not protect us. We will not fight and kill other people of color in the world who, like black people, are being victimized by the white racist government of America. We will protect ourselves from the force and violence of the racist police and the racist military, by whatever means necessary.

7. We want an immediate end to POLICE BRUTALITY and MURDER of black people.
 We believe we can end police brutality in our black community by organizing black self-defense groups that are dedicated to defending our black community from racist police oppression and brutality. The Second Amendment to the Constitution of the United States gives a right to bear arms. We therefore believe that all black people should arm themselves for self-defense.

8. We want freedom for all black men held in federal, state, county and city prisons and jails.
 We believe that all black people should be released from the many jails and prisons because they have not received a fair and impartial trial.

9. We want all black people when brought to trial to be tried in court by a jury of their peer group or people from their black communitites, as defined by the Constitution of the United States.
 We believe that the courts should follow the United States Constitution so that black people will receive fair trials. The 14th Amendment of the U.S. Constitution gives a man a right to be tried by his peer group. To do this the court will be forced to select a jury from the black community from which the black defendant came. We have been, and are being tried by all-white juries that have no understanding of the "average reasoning man" of the black community.

10. We want land, bread, housing, education, clothing, justice and peace. And as our major political objective, a United Nations-supervised plebiscite to be held throughout the black colony in which only black colonial subjects will be allowed to participate, for the purpose of determining the will of black people as to their national destiny.

THE COMMITTEE TO DEFEND THE PANTHER 21
is in urgent need of
volunteer workers and funds

Call or write now to say that you will help

Address
37 Union Square West, New York, NY 10003
Telephone
243-2260 or 243-2261

Committee to Defend the Black Panther 21, *Serve the People: Black Panther Party Platform and Program*, printed in *The Black Panther* (Oakland, CA), newspaper, 1969/1970.

FORUM:
MALCOLM X FILM: THE STRUGGLE FOR FREEDOM
PANEL: MICHAEL WARREN, lawyer for Michael Stewart
family; AHMED OBAFEMI, New Afrikan Independence
Movement; JOHN BROWN ANTI-KLAN COMMITTEE;
Questions & Answers

SATURDAY, FEB. 25 7 PM 85 E. 4TH ST.
UKRAINIAN LABOR HOME/ between 1st & 2nd Aves., Manhattan
$3.00 donation requested childcare

DEMONSTRATION:
STOP KILLER COPS!
REMEMBER MICHAEL STEWART!
MONDAY, FEB. 27 5:00-6:00 PM
14TH ST. & 1ST AVE.

THE POLICE ARE AN OCCUPYING ARMY
IN THE BLACK COMMUNITY.
—MALCOLM X

SPONSORED BY JOHN BROWN ANTI-KLAN COMMITTEE P.O. BOX 406, NYC 10009, 989-8898

LIVING UNDER DISINVESTMENT: WHOSE STREETS? OUR STREETS!

In the late 1970s and early 1980s, American inner cities were struggling with deindustrialization, massive unemployment, and a collapsing tax base. Rather than deal with these root problems, a national consensus emerged that punitive measures were the best way to address rising crime rates. Calls to "get tough on crime" and "lock them up" were parroted by the media and popularized across the country. The fact that the victims of the rise in crime were almost entirely from the communities being criminalized didn't deter most of white, middle-class America from embracing racism and claiming that crime was one of the most important national issues to be addressed.

Progressive urban policies won by Civil Rights organizations in the previous decades were defunded and overturned in cities across the country in favor of increased police presence—and a commensurate increase in incarceration. Law enforcement and prison budgets ballooned, which did little to address crime but massively increased violence in poor and working class communities. In response, and after an explosion of high-profile killings by police in the 1980s (including Eleanor Bumpurs and Michael Stewart in New York City), organizations and activists mobilized to address violence and poverty in their own neighborhoods.

(Left) John Brown Anti-Klan Committee, *Stop Killer Cops! Remember Michael Stewart!* (New York, NY), flier, 1984. The John Brown Anti-Klan Committee was an organization of white anti-racists and prison abolitionists formed in 1977 in response to rising white nationalist organizing inside and outside of America's prisons and the resurgence of the Ku Klux Klan.

Mariame Kaba, founder of Project NIA and Survived & Punished, reflects on her first realization of the way police target young people:

"I became interested and radicalized around state violence through the violence of policing. My first memory of that was the killing of Michael Stewart in 1983 in New York City, where I grew up. It was the first time that I realized very clearly that cops killed Black people like me. I think it was because he was young-ish. I was 12 and he was 25, but he was a young person in my eyes.

I remember older family and friends being very agitated about what had happened. Where I grew up in the East Village, a lot of young people were doing graffiti work. Michael Stewart was purportedly tagging when the police killed him. It felt relatable. I have a very vivid memory of that particular incident, and that was the first anti-police violence protest that I attended. That was also very significant. I had never actually gone on my own and with friends to a protest before. That was my first one."

Buttons, left to right: *A Day of Remembrance: Nicholas Naquan Heyward Jr., Not in Vain; Remember Michael Stewart* (New York, NY), n.d.

THE MICHAEL STEWART
MURDER AND COVERUP

Remember Michael Stewart

Pages 21-24: Michael Stewart Legal Defense Fund Committee, *Remember Michael Stewart* (New York, NY), pamphlet, 1983/1984.

On September 15, 1983, Michael Stewart was beaten into a coma by 11 New York City transit police officers. He died 13 days later. While his death may not be that unusual—179 people were slain by NYC police between 1978 and 1982, all but 36 of them either Black or Hispanic—the case points not only to police misconduct but also to a conspiracy involving the Transit Police, the Medical Examiner, the District Attorney, and ultimately the mayor and the governor.

While Stewart's family has battled for over a year to discover how their son died and who was responsible, each of these officials and agencies has contributed to the continuing effort to cover up evidence of police racism and use of deadly force.

Twenty-five-year-old Stewart was on his way home to Brooklyn just after 2 AM when he was arrested for allegedly writing on the wall. The arresting officer was white. Stewart was Black. With his hands cuffed behind his back, Stewart was taken to the street, where four white backup cops joined them. Once there, according to witnesses, one of the cops lifted Stewart off the ground by his clothes. After severely beating him around the head, the cop dropped Stewart to the pavement, causing his head to slam against the concrete. He

then was packed into a police van and driven to the station house, where witnesses saw several policemen beat him again with their nightsticks. When he finally fell to the ground, he was kicked repeatedly until his screams became inaudible. At that point Stewart was "hogtied" (his ankles and wrists drawn together behind his back), thrown into another van and taken to Bellevue Hospital.

At five a.m. that same morning, two policemen informed Mr. and Mrs. Stewart that their son was in the hospital. After two hours of pressuring hospital officials, they were informed that their son was lying in a coma, fighting for his life. At that point, the Stewarts and their attorney (who the Stewarts contacted as soon as they heard about their son), requested that their own physician, Dr. Robert Wolff, be allowed to examine him. When the Stewarts finally got to see their son (at this point learning he was in police custody), the signs of his beating were clearly visible.

By September 28, the day Michael Stewart died, his family and their lawyers had begun to piece together a picture of what had happened. After his initial examination, Dr. Wolff had concluded that Stewart had suffered a severe beating. From the hemorrhaging of his eyes and a compression at his neck, Wolff was fairly certain that Stewart had been strangled. The family then called in their own forensic pathologist, Dr. John Grauerholz, to oversee the autopsy which was to take place the next day.

The autopsy was conducted by New York City's chief medical examiner, Dr. Elliott Gross, who found that "Michael Stewart died of cardiac arrest." Beyond confirming that Stewart died because his heart stopped beating, Gross's report contended that "there was no evidence of physical injury resulting in or contributing to death."

The veracity of these conclusions was immediately challenged by Dr. Wolff and Dr. Grauerholz. They charged that Stewart's death resulted from "20-30 seconds of pressure to his neck," which was "compressed by applied pressure from the front or side . . . by another person or persons." In other words, Stewart had been strangled. Grauerholz concluded that the death "should have been classified a homicide."

Two days after Gross's official report, without the family's knowledge and in direct violation of their agreement and the law, Gross removed Stewart's eyes and placed them in a bottle of formaldehyde solution, effectively washing out any signs of hemorrahging.

This evidence of a medical coverup further fueled charges of police brutality and racism in the Stewart case. As pressure continued to mount Gross was forced to conduct a second autopsy. In his final report, he revised his findings to observe that Stewart had suffered over 60 bruises to his head, face, neck and other extremities. He further stated: "Michael Stewart collapsed while in police custody and died from physical injury to the spinal cord and neck."

The level of public outrage in the Black community was such that Manhattan District Attorney Robert Morgenthau was compelled to convene a grand jury investigation on October 25, over a month after the incident. As if to prove his bad faith, and to broaden the developing conspiracy, Morgenthau's first act was to grant immunity from prosecution to eight of the 11 transit cops involved in Stewart's death. The remaining three were charged with felony misdemeanor. Six months after the grand jury convened, its deliberations ended resulting in an indictment of the three. However, a judge threw out the indictments because of alleged misconduct by one of the grand jurors, Ronald P. Fields. Fields, the judge charged, had tried to conduct his own investigation and had shared his findings with others on the panel.

Although the Stewart family has pressed for the appointment of a special prosecutor since November of 1983, and despite their presenting Governor Cuomo with petitions in support of their call, Cuomo has refused to appoint a special prosecutor, claiming that he wants first to see the results of all pending court actions.

The significance of the Michael Stewart case lies in the exposure of the conspiratorial relationship between the district attorney, the medical examiner and the police, with at least the tacit approval and cooperation of the mayor and governor. The existence of such a relationship isn't new, as evidenced by the fact that only one police officer has been convicted for killing a civilian in the last 25 years. Countless numbers, including Arthur Miller, Randolph Evans, and Luis Baez, to name only a few, have been victims of racist police brutality.

Mayor Ed Koch, already regarded as a virulent racist by the city's Black community, faces a campaign for reelection in 1985. The continuing scandal of the Stewart case could have a major impact on that race. In addition, Governor Cuomo, a man who literally owes his job to the overwhelming support he received from Black voters, may also find himself in hot water as a result of his refusal to apoint a special prosecutor.

The Michael Stewart Legal Defense Fund Committee is a coalition of individuals and organizations working to raise funds for and to inform people about the campaign to expose the truth and win justice in the case of the murder of Michael Stewart.

YOU CAN HELP!

Please fill out this coupon and send it to:

MSLDFC, 75 Maple St., Bklyn, NY 11225

Make checks payable to the Michael Stewart Legal Defense Fund Committee.

_____ I would like to work with the Committee

_____ Please put me on your mailing list and keep me informed of developments in the Michael Stewart case.

_____ Enclosed is my contribution of $____ to help in this fight for justice.

NAME _____

ADDRESS _____

_____ Zip _____

PHONE _____

DAY OF OUTRAGE *continues...*

NO JUSTICE NO PEACE!

JANUARY 21 ANNIVERSARY RALLY

Governor Cuomo & Mayor Koch, along with Uncle Tom Ben Ward's racist police continue to disrespect and kill Black People Daily

IN '88, WE DEMAND THE FOLLOWING:

1. *Amnesty for the 73 arrested December 21, 1987.*
2. *Immediate arrest of the Transit Authority cops named in the illegal arrest of Black and Latino people.*
3. *The Goshen 4: John Hassel, John Melvin, Jose Roch, Olio Serrano; brothers in the Orange County Jail under attack and threat of assassination by the KKK—transferred to the MCC.*
4. *Hands off Twawana Brawley; appointment of a a special investigator in the case—specifically Basil Patterson.*
5. *Immediate arrest and suspension of the Police who killed Alfred Sanders, Yvonne Smallwood and Ken Roy Burke.*

Return to Columbus Plaza, Brooklyn (off Myrtle and Jay)

THURSDAY, JANUARY 21, 1988—3 PM

BRING TOKENS (A, F, 2, 3, 4, & 5 to Borough Hall)

On toward the General Strike!

SPONSORED BY THE DECEMBER 12TH COMMITTEE—(718) 712-5447

The December 12th Committee, *Day of Outrage continues* (Brooklyn, NY), poster, 1988.

Civilian Watch Groups

While cities were struggling with unemployment and the national economic downturn, the crack epidemic was also ravaging communities. Law enforcement treated the rise in addiction and crime as another reason to harass people of color, and communities were forced to develop their own methods to deal with the epidemic. The direct-action organization Black Men's Movement Against Crack in New York, founded by activist Sonny Carson, educated youth about drug safety and created citizen-patrol groups in Bed-Stuy, Harlem, and the Bronx. Carson and the group's members claimed that the NYPD did nothing to prevent the spread of crack and that police were in fact often working with and profiting off of drug dealers. The Mollen Commission, known formally as the Commission to Investigate Allegations of Police Corruption and the Anti-Corruption Procedures of the Police Department, released a report in 1993 that confirmed widespread criminality within the NYPD and that officers were stealing and selling drugs and protecting dealers.

White flight to suburban areas coincided with a rise in white violence against Black men and women. In the late 1980s, groups including the Racist Violence Response Network, the Committee Against Police Violence, and CAAAV (the Committee Against Anti-Asian Violence) organized together after a group of white teens murdered Michael Griffith—a 23-year-old Trinidadian man—in Howard Beach and, a few years later, when 16-year-old Yusef Hawkins was attacked by a mob of white teens in Bensonhurst, Brooklyn. The Network created phone trees to report and respond to "racist terror" by police and white bigots in the city.

Asian American communities across the country formed anti-violence groups following the killing of Vincent Chin in 1982. Chin was murdered in a suburb outside of Detroit by two unemployed autoworkers who mistakenly believed he was Japanese and blamed America's declining auto industry on Japanese imports. A lack of police interest in the case, combined with emerging recognition of the racial bias and violence faced by Asians in Detroit and elsewhere, led to the creation of groups like American Citizens for Justice (Detroit), Asian Americans Advancing Justice (Los Angeles), and Asians for Justice (Boston) to tackle racial discrimination and police violence against racialized minorities head-on. In New York City, CAAAV was organized after a 1986 forum on "Violence Against Asians in America" and it began to track police violence against Asian Americans while also organizing to support immigrant and refugee victims of police brutality in court and in the streets.

Not all of the groups organized to defend communities were strictly anti-police. Civilian volunteer groups like the city-funded Angels' Night in Detroit kept watch for vandalism and Curtis Sliwa's Guardian Angels, who patrolled the subway with their signature red berets, represented a "tough on crime" alternative and had more than 700 volunteers at its height. These vigilante organizations capitalized on the growing fear of mostly suburban whites that integrated cities were becoming more dangerous and under-policed.

WHAT IS THE TRUE "DANGER TO BLACK YOUTH"?

CHECK OUT THE FACTS

Pages 27-30: Black Men's Movement Against Crack, *What is the True "Danger to Black Youth"?* (Brooklyn, NY), pamphlet, 1986.

What is the "Danger to Our Youth?"

On Wednesday, December 10, 1986, the Black Men's Movement Against Crack was barred from P.S. 335 where we were to hold our regular weekly meeting on eliminating crack from our communities and calling for *Death to the Crack Dealers*! Some twenty to twenty-five members of the P.T.A. of P.S. 335 went to the District Superintendent's office, Ms. Joyce Coppin, who had P.S. 335 closed and successfully sabotaged the meeting.

All of this was engineered by the police, the 77th Precinct, the FBI-NYPD Joint Terrorist Task Force and Mayor Koch's Anti-Crack Task Forces

WHY?

Black Men's Movement Against Crack	*Police and their Weapons*
February 1986 - raised the epidemic proportion of the 'Crack Menace'. Mother-in-law, (Mrs. Chambers), of one of its members brutally killed by 'crack head'.	*Murdered* Eleanor Bumpurs. No arrest. February - dormant on crack issue; murder of Mrs. Chambers never solved.
Every week through February, March, April -marched, organized, held mass community meetings in many Bed-Stuy public schools.	Police Community Relations tried to send in provocateurs and disrupters.
June, July, August - raised the real solution to dope in our communities 'recapture our communities by any means necessary.'	Increased presence on the street - harassed masses of our people. *Murdered* Dennis Groce.
July - Black Power Rally Against Crack, 500 people march and close crack paraphenalia stores.	Police intervene on behalf of crack stores. Place provocateurs inside march.
Close Crack house on Kosciusko Street.	Police respond to call by crack dealers, threaten people in march; Captain of 77th Precinct says Black Men's Movement are 'vigilantes' and must be stopped.

Black Men's Movement goes to the Bronx and Harlem to give support to people fighting against crack.

Two brothers from the Black Men's Movement arrested by overkill, zealous police. Label Black Men's Movement as 'violent'.

Raises police protection of Crack dealers; police precinct as undercover crack house.

77th Precinct exposed due to Black Men's Movement work. Not one member of the P.T.A. of P.S. 335 nor Ms. Coppin's office participated.

Increased participation by masses of Black people.

Black people increase street protest marches and demonstrations.

Police presence as an occupying force increases - many traffic violations cited. Obviously mentally handicapped people jostled, manhandled and thrown into police cars as the police attempt to take control of the streets.

Raise 'crack as chemical warfare against our people.'

FBI and NYPD Joint Terrorist Task Force summoned - counter-insurgency tactics commence. Crack houses in and around all public schools flourish.

Black Men's Movement under police surveillance.

Willing dupes (weapons), point at movement to close the crack houses as the problem, as opposed to police, chickens, crack dealers.

Demand 77th Precinct closed - community mobilized for demonstration at precinct.

Dope dealing scandal spreads - Ward "77th Precinct is the scandal, will transfer all."

Cops rebel - Blue Flu. Crack houses flourish; murders, atrocities increase.

Organize Harvey Brown Brigade for youth. Establish positive image for young Black men.

Organize teach out at Boys ' Girls High School.

Koch, Ward appear at Boys - Girls High School to minimize effect of Black Men's Movement Against Crack political education and grassroots organizing.

Assault, then arrest or kill, many, many Larry Davises.

Establish positive image in community as Black men willing to put their very lives in danger to rid the community of crack, occupying forces of corrupt police, chickens and all those who benefit from the chemical warfare called "dope".

Organize most backward sector of community to misidentify the "enemy", "the danger to our youth".

Enlist Black informers in the move to destroy the credibility of the Black Men's Movement Against Crack.

Murdered Michael Stewart.

The past 10 months Black Men have organized over 48 demonstrations every Saturday, putting between 20 to 50 men on the street every Saturday.

Distributed over 300,000 leaflets to the community urging Black people to join and to resist crack dealers and police protection thereof - organized town meetings every Wednesday for last 10 months - over 10,000 people attended.

WHO ARE THE REAL ENEMIES

and

WHAT IS THE REAL DANGER TO BLACK YOUTH?

2018.034

Pages 31-33: Racist Violence Response Network, *Racist Violence Response Network* (New York, NY), brochure, 1986.

WHAT IS THE RACIST VIOLENCE RESPONSE NETWORK?

The Racist Violence Response Network (RVRN) has been formed to protest and call attention to racist attacks by police and white mobs in New York City.

Although the December 1986 attack in Howard Beach, Queens, made headlines, racist violence has in fact been an historical and pervasive reality in New York City. Today, Black, Latino, and Asian New Yorkers are being attacked by police and white mobs with increasing frequency.

Most reporting of racist violence is buried in back pages of newspapers, if covered at all. Rarely do racist attackers pay for their crimes, either in the courts or by public condemnation. This green light for racist violence must cease.

The burden of protesting racist violence has been carried by Black, Latino and Asian communities. It is time for white people to stand up and actively confront the racist violence emanating from the white community. Violent mobs, killer cops and complacent citizenry should no longer define white New Yorkers. White people opposed to racist violence can no longer be silent, but must actively demonstrate and vocalize opposition.

The Racist Violence Response Network acts to expose the prevalence of racist violence and to generate a climate of condemnation and outrage against such racist terror, particularly within the white community. The Response Network is a vehicle specifically, but not exclusively, for white people to generate awareness in the white community in order to intensify pressure on public officials, the courts, the media and other institutions to stop the racist bloodshed on New York City streets.

CONTEXT OF RACIST VIOLENCE

Racist violence occurs within the broader context of institutionalized racism in society at large. Though African, Latino, Asian, Arab and Native Americans constitute a majority in New York City, political and economic power remain largely in white hands.

■ A white dominated school system with 80% Black, Latino and Asian students, fails to educate over half of them while "educating" many of the white youths participating in racist mob violence.

■ A white dominated real estate industry gentrifies Black and Latino neighborhoods into enclaves of white privilege, while turning tens of thousands onto the streets and into squalid welfare hotels and shelters.

■ Unemployment rates of Black and Latino New Yorkers remain twice those of white, while one half of Black and Latino children live in poverty.

■ Cutbacks in city social services have been matched by Reaganomic's slashing of social programs to fuel U.S. militarism abroad and tax cuts for the wealthy at home.

■ White supremacy resurges nationally, from the racist policies of the White House to paramilitary terrorist groups, such as the KKK and Aryan Nations.

■ White racist violence escalates along with rape and battering of women of all colors, violence and vandalism against Jews, and "queer-bashing" against lesbians and gay men.

■ This is the context in which Black, Latino and Asian New Yorkers are being brutalized by white mobs and cops. White people have a particular responsibility to fight racist violence in the streets while we collaborate with other communities in their struggles for empowerment. By unified action, we can overturn institutional polices and practices.

WHAT IS RACIST VIOLENCE?

Racist violence, and racism in general, involves the power of one racial group to impose its will and policies on disempowered racial groups. Power in all segments of New York City has historically rested in the white community and is still denied to people of color.

White racist violence is perpetrated spontaneously by mobs and vigilantes, or systemically by cops. Over 250 people of color have been killed by New York City cops during Mayor Koch's ten years in office since 1977. Such violence persists because racist actions are condoned and covered up by the white controlled police forces, prosecutors, medical examiners, governmental administrations, courts, media and all other institutions of power.

RESPONSE TO RACIST VIOLENCE

The Response Network has established a phone tree for mobilizing timely and effective responses to outbreaks of racist violence in New York City. When a racist attack occurs, the Response Network becomes activated in consultation with activists in the Black, Latino, or Asian community affected.

Individuals and organizations that have submitted their names to the phone tree are called upon to participate in a concerted public response. This might involve a demonstration or vigil at the scene of the attack, at a police station or at some other appropriate locale; a letter writing or phone calling campaign; or other creative responses that benefit by a rapid mobilization.

If you or your organization wish to be involved in this effort to stop racist violence, please fill out and send in the attached form.

☐ Yes, add my name and phone number to the Response Network.

☐ Yes, I will help you organize the Response Network.

☐ Enclosed is a donation of $_____ to help this project. (Make checks payable to RVRN.)

☐ Contact me with more information.

Name: _____ Organization: _____

Address: _____

Phone: Day: _____ Evening: _____ Zip: _____

RETURN TO: RVRN, 1560 Broadway, Room 807, Box 18, New York, New York 10036

BICYCLIST SAYS OFFICERS BEAT HIM AS THEY HELD HIM IN TRAFFIC CASE

From a New York Times article, Sept. 6, 1987

The police are investigating a Queens man's charge that two officers beat him Friday as they arrested him for riding his bicycle against rush-hour traffic in mid-Manhattan.

In telephone interviews yesterday, several witnesses corroborated the complaint of the victim, Ou Young, 20 years old, of Elmhurst, Queens, who said the officers pulled him violently from his bicycle, forced him to the pavement and beat him.

"One cop looked like he was trying to break his arm, and the other was almost on top of him," said one of the witnesses, Sharon Holmquist, 25, of Queens.

She said that as Mr. Ou screamed for help, he was "being crunched up on the street while they banged his head on the ground."

In a telephone interview, Mr. Ou acknowledged that he did not have any identification with him at the time of the incident and said he was surprised when one of the officers "gave me a push off the bike."

Mr. Ou, said the police called him "scum" and told him "if you don't cooperate, you're going to jail."

He said that when he replied "Let's go there, I know my rights," the officers pushed him to the pavement and began to hit him.

Ellen Texeira, a witness who lives near the site of the incident, said the officers appeared to become violent when Mr. Ou failed to let go of his bicycle.

At that point, she said, one of the officers "threw him on the pavement," while the other began punching him in the back."

Ms. Texeira said that when onlookers began screaming "Stop it! Stop it!," to the police, they stopped hitting him and handcuffed him.

Ms. Texeira said that Mr. Ou was bruised on the neck and bleeding from the right arm when he got up. She said she told him to try to calm down and was warned by one of the officers, "If you open your mouth once more I'm going to put you with him."

Mr. Ou is a Korean who has lived in the United States for three years.

The police said that Mr. Ou was charged with traffic violations, disorderly conduct and obstructing governmental administration.

EWGAPA REPRESENTATIVES

American Baptist Churches
Walter Owyang
1365 Altschul Ave.
Menlo Park, CA 94025

American Citizens for Justice
Kim Bridges
2336 Greensboro
Troy, MI 48098

Asian Pacific American Legal Center
Stewart Kwoh
1010 S. Flower St., Rm. 302
Los Angeles, CA 90015

Break the Silence
Rachel Shigekane
310 Eighth St., #205
Oakland, CA 94607

Episcopal Church
Magdaleno Bacagan
1116 W. 141st St.
Gardena, CA 90247

Friends Service Committee
Ed Nakawatase
1501 Cherry St.
Philadelphia, PA 19102

Christian Church (Disciples of Christ)
Gerald Cunningham
P.O. Box 1986
Indianapolis, IN 46206

Presbyterian Church (USA)
Paul Louie
1648 Redcliff Rd.
Los Angeles, CA 90026
Wesley Woo
475 Riverside Dr. #1244
New York, NY 10115

Lutheran Church of America
Cynthia Luft
231 Madison Ave.
New York, NY 10016

Reformed Church in America
Ella White
356 Maple Hill Dr.
Hackensack, NJ 07601

United Church of Christ
Rita Inoway
885 First Ave.
Salt Lake City, UT 84103

Miya Okawara
447 19th Ave.
San Francisco, CA 94121

United Methodist Church
Moses Lee
475 Riverside Dr. #329
New York, NY 10115

What is EWGAPA?

The Ecumenical Working Group of Asian and Pacific Americans (EWGAPA) was formed in response to needs articulated at a national consultation of church leaders concerned with and about Asian and Pacific Americans. This December 1984 meeting focused on racially motivated violence against Asian and Pacific Americans. The original EWGAPA consisted of representatives from nine denominations and three community groups: American Baptist Churches, Episcopal, Friends, Christian Church (Disciples of Christ), Presbyterian Church (USA), Reformed Church in America, Lutheran Church of America, United Church of Christ, United Methodist Churches, American Citizens for Justice, Asian Pacific American Legal Center, and the Asian Pacific Racial Justice Network of Northern California. Since its inception, Break the Silence has replaced Racial Justice Network as our liaison group in northern California. EWGAPA will conclude its third year of a three-year commitment in 1988. The group meets twice annually and sees its purpose to be the enabling of its constituencies to combat racially motivated violence against Asians and Pacific Islanders.

2018.039

Ecumenical Working Group of Asian and Pacific Americans, "Bicyclist says officers beat him as they held him in traffic case," *EWGAPA News* (New York, NY), newsletter, Winter 1988.

Citywide Committee Against
Police And Racial Violence

WHAT YOU CAN DO:
IF YOU ARE THE VICTIM OF
POLICE ABUSE

or
If you witness an Incident of
Police Violence!

CALL THE
COMMITTEE
AGAINST POLICE
VIOLENCE
(718) 953-8411

YOUR RIGHTS
ON THE STREET
IN A CAR
AT HOME
AT THE POINT OF
ARREST

They have the authority to investigate the incident and bring State or Federal Criminal charges respectively against the officer(s).

WHO WE ARE

The Committee Against Police and Racial Violence is composed of community activists, lawyers, law students, photographers, doctors and other resource people who are concerned about the rise of police violence in our communities. It has organized seminars and training workshops, monitoring of trials, demonstrations and other activities which seek to coordinate the community's response to incidents of police violence. This pamphlet was created to provide information and guidance to individuals who have or witness a confrontation with the police. Please share it with others. Additional copies are available from:

**Center For Law And Social Justice
of Medgar Evers College
1473 Fulton Street
Brooklyn, New York 11216**
JOIN NOW!

2018.039

Citywide Committee Against Police and Racial Violence, *What You Can Do if You Are the Victim of Police Abuse* (Brooklyn, NY), brochure, n.d.

Community Meeting to Protest Racist Violence and Police Brutality

On March 20, 1987 on West 93rd st. in full view of his neighbors, Alberto Flores was handcuffed and beaten by the N.Y.C. police. A neighbor, Rafael Escano, videotaped the beating and shortly afterwards the video was shown on T.V. It clearly showed that the police had lied when they denied beating Alberto Flores. But despite the video, Alberto Flores was indicted by a grand jury in late May for resisting arrest and assalting an officer. The District Attorney said that there wasn't enough evidence to charge the police.

- **See the unedited video of the Police beating of Alberto Flores**
- **Hear testimony from victims of racist violence**
- **Hear speakers on the anti-racist fightback**

Whether we are Puerto Rican, Dominican, Latino, Black or Asian, being beaten by the police or a racist mob is nothing new for us in this country. A short time before Michael Griffith was chased to his death by a racist mob in Queens last December, a Puerto Rican and a Dominican youth were beaten a few blocks away. Two weeks later in the Bronx, 8 transit police beat 2 young Puerto Rican women while calling them Spiks and Dykes. And in January of this year a Cuban man, Alberto Lana, was shot to death in the Bronx by a cop over a parking space.

While the number of racial attacks is clearly growing both in New York and throughout the U.S., the failure of our political leaders (from Ronald Reagan to Ed Koch) to strongly denounce and act against racism has given the racists a green light to continue their actions. Skyrocketing rents, displacement, the end of affirmative action, the anti-immigration laws and the English Only movement are all part of the UPSURGE OF RACISM IN THIS COUNTRY!!

Racism in America has always been used to divide poor and working people. As Puerto Ricans, Dominicans, and other Latinos we must unite our communities and join together with Blacks, Asians and progressive Whites to fight for an end to racial violence.

Thursday, July 2, 7 p.m.
at the Community Center, 647 Columbus Ave.
(between 91st & 92nd Streets)

Organizers: Latino Coalition for Racial Justice (All People's Congress, Association of Puerto Rican Executive Directors, Community Association of Progressive Dominicans, Latinos United for Political Action, National Congress for Puerto Rican Rights, Northern Manhattan Coalition for Immigrants Rights, Puerto Rican Committee Against Repression, Puerto Rican Legal Defense Fund).
Endorsers: Asociacion de Dominicanos Progresistas, Bloque Socialists, C.E.D.U.C.A., N.Y.C. Dominican Action Committee, Nuevo Horizontes Latinoamericano, Partido de Trabajadores Dominicanos, Rev. Roberto Morales, Colectiva de Mujeres Dominicanas, Harlem Committee Against Racist Violence and Police Repression.

Latino Coalition for Racial Justice, Community Meeting to Protest Racist Violence and Police Brutality (New York, NY), flier, 1987.

Buttons, left to right: *Stop the Rise of Police Violence: Justice for Eleanor Bumpurs; No Excuses for Police Brutality: Justice for Amadou Diallo* (New York, NY), n.d.

$1.25 • NOVEMBER 24, 1980

Four Hot New Designers, by Caterine Milinaire
Of Bones, Cancer, and Money, by Lally Weymouth

NEW YORK

The Guardian Angels
A Help–or a Hype? By Nicholas Pileggi

New York magazine (New York, NY), November 24, 1980.

Mariame Kaba

Interviewed by JOSH MACPHEE

Mariame Kaba is an organizer, educator, curator, and prison industrial complex (PIC) abolitionist who is active in movements for racial, gender, and transformative justice.

JOSH MACPHEE: We've been working on a project around the history of policing and opposition to police violence and racist policing, and the intersection of these issues. To start off, could you share where you connect to this history? What do you see as your lineage in this work, and where do you personally step into this timeline of struggle?

MARIAME KABA: I became interested and radicalized around state violence through the violence of policing. My first memory of that was the killing of Michael Stewart in 1983 in New York City, where I grew up. It was the first time that I realized very clearly that cops killed Black people like me. I think it was because he was young-ish. I was 12 and he was 25, but he was a young person in my eyes. I remember older family and friends being very agitated about what had happened. Where I grew up in the East Village, a lot of young people were doing graffiti work. Michael Stewart was purportedly tagging when the police killed him. It felt relatable. I have a very vivid memory of that particular incident, and that was the first anti-police violence protest that I attended. That was also very significant. I had never actually gone on my own and with friends to a protest before. That was my first one.

And then just a couple years after that, when I had already begun anti-racist work with other people my age, I started forming groups/activist space as a young person myself.

When the MOVE bombing occurred in Philadelphia, that was another shock to my system. I couldn't believe Black people were bombed in a city so close to mine. These were people who looked like me. It was so visceral. It wasn't until later that I understood what political prisoners were, and I got involved in thinking about prisons differently. What came first was policing and the violence of it.

JM: So this became something that you were aware of in a very profound and embodied way in the 80s, and you started focusing your attention and work on this a decade or so later. Could you talk about how you started to put yourself into the story?

MK: I feel like I was always in the story in some specific way, because I had family and my brother was targeted a lot by cops. When I started, I began to organize, still as a teenager. We always included the violence of policing within those formations.

I launched Project NIA in 2009; that was really the first time my work and my job overlapped in any way. That was the first time I got paid for doing any organizing work. I was in my late 30s by that time. In Chicago at the time, I noticed a disconnect between policy and the direct community, and particularly the young people who I was in community with, who didn't really get to weigh in on the policies that were impacting their lives in such massive ways. Project NIA was an attempt to help support and create leadership pipelines for young people, particularly those who were impacted by the criminal punishment system, to have a voice in determining their own fates. Police violence was a huge part of that. They were always harassed, targeted, and violated by police.

I moved from New York to Chicago in '95. And I was struck when I arrived in Chicago at how disconnected the work of the organizers in communities of color was from what young people said they were most facing, in terms of the harassment and the targeting and the violence of the cops. I remember the stories that were told to me by young folks who would say: the cops pick us up and drop us off in rival gang territory and tell us, "Good luck making it back." I remember going to meetings and having none of that come up when we were talking about race, racism, community violence, community safety strategies. I started Project NIA because I thought: something else is needed here that also supports the organizing capacity of young people.

I'll just backtrack for one second to say something about how Chicago was termed "the false confession capital of the US," and is the home of [police detective and commander] Jon Burge and his "Midnight Crew." So many Black folks were engaged in organizing to make the Burge cases known, and to get justice for the survivors and for the people who didn't make it through that.

I want to be clear that I'm not making the case that people weren't organizing against the violence of policing or the criminal punishment system. When I came to Chicago in '95, Burge had been fired two years earlier. I had not been involved in organizing to get Burge fired because by the time I showed up, he'd already been fired. There was ongoing organizing to get people off death row who had been put there by him and his henchmen. But, by the time I came to an abolitionist politic in the late 90s, I was not in support of the organizing that was focused on finding ways to incarcerate the cops who had caused this deep harm. I couldn't reconcile that with my politics, so I was always adjacent to that work. It wasn't until 2010 when Burge was finally convicted in federal court for lying about torture, and the community was deflated after that "win," that I saw an opportunity to engage on that particular effort.

I saw an opportunity to re-engage in that fight, but to think about how we might do that differently, through an abolitionist lens instead. Could there be something restorative here, something transformative? I was asked to be on the advisory board of the Chicago Torture Justice Memorials. I bring that up because a big part of how that work came together also overlapped with We Charge Genocide, which was a youth-led intergenerational effort that I co-founded to get a group of young Black and Brown people to the UN in Geneva, to make the case against the torture of police in Chicago.

We Charge originated after we lost Damo [Dominic Franklin Jr.], who had been getting involved in Circles & Ciphers with Project NIA. He was tased and killed by the cops. That was in May of 2014, a few months before Mike Brown was killed in Ferguson.

I say all this to say: some of the things that happen in the organizing work that you do are less about predicting what is going to happen, and more about reacting to the things that are going on. But that only works when there's a foundation that existed before through which you can actually take your ideas and move them to the next level. The 30 years of folks struggling to make the Burge cases legible to the broader public—we stepped into that 30 years later. That was very important as to why we ended up winning reparations. We need to think about the lineages of these things in the long view. Our wins are not our wins alone; we are building off legacies, even of peoples' struggles and tactics that we didn't politically agree with.

These things don't just materialize out of thin air, they're built off of a trajectory of the years that came before.

I wanted to put that into the mix, because it's really critically important to me. Defund comes out of somewhere too. Like [former Black Panther and political prisoner] Eddie Ellis who articulated an "invest/divest" frame in the 1990s. These things don't just materialize out of thin air, they're built off of a trajectory of the years that came before. And they're also often a response to what didn't work earlier.

I've talked to younger organizers who said, "well, the invest/divest framework comes from the Vision for Black Lives that came out in 2016," and I'm like, of course not. Of course not. Yes, that got codified in a certain way, and it got taken up by people in a certain way. But in the late 90s or maybe early 2000s, I heard Eddie Ellis constantly saying that we've got to invest in communities and divest from these systems that are killing us.

These things don't just materialize from nothing.

I do believe in the idea that spontaneous uprisings do happen and push people. But there is usually something that came before to build on. I think those work symbiotically. This is part of those decades of work that I talked about: that no one saw, and that was not sexy. People were just in their communities toiling away for years with very little resources, and now people are ready to listen. That's the point. This is part of why there really isn't one beginning and certainly not one end. There is always work. There is always organizing, there is always something happening where people are trying to be ready for whenever there are opportunities for people to take up new demands.

I know you also asked about Survived & Punished, and I can quickly talk about that.

We founded Survived & Punished in late 2015. It's a formation of defense campaigns that came together because we had been individually working on defense campaigns for survivors of gender-based violence of various kinds, and trying to create opportunities for those survivors to either be let out of prison or jail, or to avoid deportation. We realized that in coming together, we would have much better chances of advancing a coherent analysis that would help more people and would amplify the voices and analyses that we were trying to get across around the criminalization of survivors, and the criminalization of survival.

So now we are a formation that includes affiliates of Survived & Punished in New York, California and Illinois. We have been working to get people out and to free survivors in multiple kinds of ways. The issue of policing obviously comes in here, because of the fact that people are arrested by cops who make decisions to arrest survivors. Policing also comes in around the issue of prosecution and law enforcement; district attorneys and prosecutors who act as cops, who criminalize survivors and survival. We center an analysis of racialized, gendered violence, making sure that people understand that that's a co-constitutive part of the prison-industrial complex. Prisons have, and will be as long as they exist, gendered institutions. We've been trying to insert that analysis throughout the work, insisting that people also pay attention to women, to gender non-conforming people.

JM: I want to talk about the question of lenses. You've become very adept and successful at using things like social media to raise awareness around issues. Could you talk a little bit about these things as tools for addressing police violence? And also the interconnections, conflicts, and missed connections between these questions of changing lenses and framing and language and kind of the sort of more traditional grassroots on the ground, analyzing and building power?

MK: I haven't spent most of my time making distinctions between "real life" and virtual. There are several reasons for that. The first is, it became pretty clear to me a few years ago how ableist our organizing strategies and spaces were, how it leaves out so many people who just can't make it to meetings from 6:30 to 9pm or 10pm at night because they have childcare and they have jobs they have to go to in the morning. My own life changed. My capacity changed and my ability to show up at every meeting changed.

I'm a Luddite, but what social media afforded me is, I use the skills I learned through community-based organizing and apply them to social media. What I learned was that if you are authentic to yourself, sharing information about things that people might be interested in, if you build a relationship of trust with people, people will respond, people will want to ask you questions, people will want to know what you think about a particular issue. All those ways that I'm a good organizer are the reason I could do social media.

What I know from organizing is you always meet people where they are, and there are a hell of a lot of people on social media. I have always used what is at my disposal to the best of my ability to connect with people and to ask people to join in, in some way. You have to give people things to do. This is something that I think is very important. People don't always know what to do.

It isn't true that people just inherently have knowledge about how to transform the conditions we're living under. It's never been true. When I was 16, knocking on doors in Harlem to get people to meetings focused on better housing, people didn't just know how to figure out how to get affordable housing. People came together. Other people who knew more came in and shared; we did political education, and we figured things out together. It was a collective process of learning and growing and knowledge building. Experience can be a teacher, but it doesn't ensure that you have an analysis of the condition that led to the bad thing happening. Unless we are working together to build collective knowledge and grow together, we're not going to. Social media is one way to build that. It's not the only way. And for some things, it's not the best way. But part of why we know so much about policing and violence right now is because of social media, and because of media in general.

NEW YORK CIVIL LIBERTIES UNION

CAMPAIGN FOR A REAL CIVILIAN COMPLAINT REVIEW BOARD

132 West 43rd Street, 2nd Floor
New York, New York 10036
(212) 382-0557

Spearheaded by the NYCLU and by New York City Council members Ronnie Eldridge, Virginia Fields, and Victor Robles, the Campaign for a Real Civilian Complaint Review Board has a broad-based coalition of supporters including 25 advocacy organizations, Congressman Ted Weiss, Senator David Paterson, Assemblyman Roger Green, 15 additional City Council members, and 16 community boards throughout New York City.

Our goal is to persuade the City Council to pass Intro. 83, a bill proposed in January 1992 that would reform Section 440 of the City Charter as it regards the Civilian Complaint Review Board (CCRB), which investigates and reviews complaints of police misconduct. Under the current law, CCRB functions are carried out in a large part by Police Department employees. We think the law should be changed to require that all members of the CCRB and its staff be civilians, without allegiances to the agency whose activities they oversee.

Specifically, Intro. 83 mandates the following:

*   *Complete separation of the CCRB from the Police Department: the reformed CCRB would be made up entirely of civilians appointed severally by the mayor, the City Council president, and the comptroller;*

*   *Appointment only of civilian professionals with no allegiances to the Police Department, as complaint investigators;*

*   *Expanded CCRB jurisdiction to include, in addition to the NYPD, the Transit, Housing, Sanitation, and Health and Hospitals Corporation police forces;*

*   *Empowering the CCRB to issue subpoenas and to requisition from law enforcement agencies copies of all reports pertaining to alleged acts of misconduct;*

*   *Public meetings twice yearly in each borough by the CCRB for the purpose of discussing its operations; and reports by the Board, monthly to the City Record and quarterly to all boroughs, indicating the number and dispositions of complaints filed;*

*   *Authorizing the CCRB to hold hearings and issue reports on individual cases, as well as on patterns, of police misconduct;*

*   *Procedural safeguards to protect the rights of those, both civilians and police, who come into contact with the CCRB.*

The new law would not change the disciplinary power of the Police Commissioner over the Police Department, or of any law enforcement agency head over that agency.

Intro. 83 will receive a hearing by the City Council's Public Safety Committee on Wednesday, September 16, 1992. If you wish to campaign for a <u>real</u> civilian complaint review board, contact Norman Siegel or Laura Murray at (212) 382-0557.

New York Civil Liberties Union, *Campaign for a Real Civilian Complaint Review Board* (New York, NY), flier, 1992.

ATTEMPTS AT REFORM

Civilian Complaint Review Board

The NYC Civilian Complaint Review Board (CCRB) was established in 1953 as an all-police oversight committee for investigating misconduct by the force in Black and Puerto Rican communities. It was formed, in part, after the NAACP revealed that the federal Justice Department had agreed to ignore any complaints lodged against the NYPD. Multiple attempts in the following years were made by the city and grassroots organizations to add actual civilians to the Review Board, but the Patrolmen's Benevolent Association (PBA) was adamant that including civilians would undermine police work and city safety. The PBA used political pressure, mounted unsuccessful lawsuits, and staged massive protests to prevent the addition of civilians to the board. After the extreme violence used by police in the 1988 Tompkins Square Park riot, public support grew for an independent, all-civilian oversight committee and, in 1993, the new review board was formed and granted subpoena power. The creation of the new committee arguably lost Mayor David Dinkins re-election, and the incoming Mayor Rudy Giuliani cut the CCRB's budget, undermining its ability to investigate complaints. During his term, Giuliani increased the NYPD budget by 35% and added 10,000 officers to the force. But the violence of the NYPD under Giuliani destabilized the city; the brutal torture of Abner Louima by police in 1997 and large protests in the Haitian community forced Giuliani to re-fund the CCRB. Groups within the force like 100 Blacks in Law Enforcement and The Latino Officers Association demanded that the department reflect the city's demographics and that the NYPD monitor units and officers that were repeatedly subjects of citizen complaints;

Citizens for Community Control (New York, NY), button, n.d.

Giuliani instead established a weakened "cultural sensitivity training" program for officers.[1] To this day, the NYPD has a pattern of withholding information, evidence, and bodycam footage from the CCRB when they are tasked with investigating misconduct. As of 2022, the CCRB remains underfunded, with a budget of $24.5 million compared to the NYPD's $6 billion.[2]

Diversifying the Force

After a number of riots in Harlem in response to police violence in the 1930s and 40s, the National Urban League and the NAACP, as well as leftist and Communist Black newspapers, called for more Black police officers in the force, especially in Harlem and other Black neighborhoods. The force at that time was less than 1% Black and the Communist-affiliated press *The People's Voice* pointed out that existing Black officers rarely rose in the ranks. As Clarence Taylor writes in his history of police brutality in New York, *Fight the Power*, the NYPD made promises to recruit more Black officers but ultimately it was the National Urban League that hosted workshops in Harlem to help would-be recruits pass the police exam.[3]

Following the riots of the summers of 1964-1967, many Northern cities elected mayors from the Black community who pledged police reform and civilian oversight. Other cities reacted with increased surveillance and police presence. Cleveland elected its first Black mayor, Carl B. Stokes, who promised to integrate the force, while Philadelphia elected notorious former police commissioner Frank Rizzo.[4] It was during this period that police departments across the country slowly began to diversify. In 1960, most departments were between 80-90% white but by the early 2000s, police demographics more closely reflected the national racial makeup, though individual departments remain not nearly as racially diverse as the communities they occupy.[5]

Currently, the NYPD is one of the most diverse forces in the nation. However, as the flier here from the Patrolmen's Benevolent Association points out, it is also now one of the lowest paid forces in the country. Non-white police officers still struggle to rise in the ranks and top positions remain overwhelmingly white. Fifteen percent of the NYPD is Black in 2022, compared to 44% white, nearly reflecting the overall demographics of the city; above the rank of captain, however, the force is still 75% white.

1   Clarence Taylor, *Fight the Power: African Americans and the Long History of Police Brutality in New York City*, NYU Press 2019, p. 184-204.
2   Eric Umansky and Molly Simon, "The NYPD Is Withholding Evidence From Investigations Into Police Abuse," *ProPublica*, August 17, 2020.
3   Taylor, p. 88.
4   Nicole Lewis, "The Kerner Omission," *The Marshall Project*, March 1, 2018.
5   Lauren Leatherby and Richard A Oppel Jr., "Which Police Departments Are as Diverse as Their Communities?," *New York Times* September 23, 2020; David Alan Sklansky, "Not Your Father's Police Department: Making Sense of the New Demographics of Law Enforcement," *Journal of Criminal Law and Criminology* 96 (3), 2006.

Alex S. Vitale, in his book *The End of Policing*, points to a number of studies that show that increasing diversity on the force does not correlate with fewer arrests or the reduction of excessive use of force in Black communities. "Even the most diverse forces have major problems with profiling and racial bias," Vitale writes, "and individual Black and Latino officers appear to perform very much like their white counterparts." [6]

Patrolmen's Benevolent Association of the City of New York, *Now that NYC cops look like this, we are among the lowest paid police officers in the country* (New York, NY), flier, 2019.

6 Alex S. Vitale, *The End of Policing,* Verso Books, 2018. p. 11.

This brochure describes some of your rights under the law when interacting with the police in New York State and offers some strategies for protecting your rights during police encounters. We know that the reality is that police officers often don't respect our rights, and that there can be a risk that asserting your rights during a police encounter may escalate the situation. Knowing your rights is critical to recognizing when they have been violated, and exercising them in the moment can help you assert them later in court. We encourage people to assert their rights calmly and respectfully and to trust their instincts to protect their safety. If you feel your rights have been violated, tell your lawyer!

"Am I free to go?"

IF A POLICE OFFICER APPROACHES AND BEGINS TO QUESTION YOU:

- Even without "reasonable suspicion," police may ask you questions.
- At this point, you can politely ask, "am I free to go?" in a calm, assertive tone. If the officer does not answer, continue to ask, "am I free to go?" or "are we free to go?"
- If the officer says, "yes," calmly walk away.
- If the officer says, "no," then you are being "stopped" or "detained."
- Police are not legally required to speak with you in your native language.
- Police are supposed to treat everyone with courtesy, professionalism and respect and should never make discriminatory or disparaging comments or remarks.

Communities United for Police Reform, *Know your Rights!* (New York, NY), pamphlet, n.d.

(Clockwise from top-left)

National Lawyers Guild, *You Have the Right to Remain Silent: A Know Your Rights Guide for Law Enforcement Encounters* (New York, NY), pamphlet, 2015.

New York Civil Liberties Union, *Know Your Rights with Police in Schools* (New York, NY), pamphlet, 2004.

Somehow I've never been stopped or frisked (New York, NY), button, n.d.

New York Civil Liberties Union, *What to do if you're stopped by the police*, RNC Edition (New York, NY), pamphlet, 2004.

Dennis Flores

Interviewed by JEN HOYER

Dennis Flores is a Nuyorican multimedia artist, activist and educator born and raised in Brooklyn. He co-founded El Grito de Sunset Park and is the lead organizer of the Sunset Park Puerto Rican Day Parade.

JEN: Could you start off by speaking a little about your own involvement with CopWatch over the years?

DENNIS: I began to document the police in 1995. It wasn't something that I was doing in an organized manner. This was instinctive, way before social media, YouTube, or any of this livestreaming cell phone technology we have today. I had a 35mm SLR camera and a tape recorder.

When I first got involved in the social justice movement, I was a member of a street organization that the administration labeled as a gang. I was 19 or 20 years old, born and raised in Sunset Park, and like many young people of color, heavily targeted by the police. As soon as I left my stoop or went to a park to meet friends there was always an encounter with the cops, on a daily basis.

Those engagements meant cops rushing us from their cars as we're hanging out. You would have this attack of cops charging you, tackling you, slamming you to the floor, and arresting you. I had no words to explain what the hell was happening to me and my peers, other than knowing instinctively that I needed to document it. I was bold enough to document cops as they approached us in this manner, photographing or tape recording them, being arrested for it dozens of times, but it became clear that this is a tactic that is keeping me safe. This is a weapon. Now, when the cops jumped at us from their cars, I dared take that bold stance and record them and hold up a tape recorder and start taking photos. That began to set a precedent and send the message. I got pounced on, beat up, or thrown in jail. But time and time again, being consistent, continuing to do this, beginning to organize myself and my friends to do this, that was a deterrent for the police.

People did this before me and after me. But in my neighborhood, I began to do this in front of others, who also took it on. It spread like wildfire.

It took years for people to finally realize: this is legal. Our own folks were scared. People were like: shut the camera off, you can't do that; the cops are gonna get us, they can arrest us, they're gonna fuck us up. Yeah, they *did* do those things. Many people looked at it like I was provoking the cops. But everybody came to learn that what I was doing was completely legal.

Our people are afraid. They're afraid to challenge, they're afraid to question. The will of our people to resist has been broken throughout the years. And there is this fear that the powers that be will "crack the whip," and put us all in line. Much like they did during times of slavery for anyone who showed any sign of resistance, to break people in.

That's what the NYPD did during the 90s to instill fear in our communities: we were afraid to go out, to smoke weed, to drink a beer, to associate, to gather, and to go against the grain and challenge what wasn't popular.

All it takes is one person to start it. El Grito created a resistance in the neighborhood where this trickled out. It created an effect in the neighborhood. There was an immediate response from the community.

The Puerto Rican Day Parade, since I can remember in the late 90s, was and is a huge parade. After the parade ended in the early evening, our community gathered and were met with over policing: they would bring in cops from all the precincts around to clean out the neighborhood. Clean out means: no Puerto Ricans in the street.

Our people will come out on a playground, guys want to play dominoes, drink a beer, smoke some weed, whatever it is that folks do when we want to celebrate. Every ethnic group is entitled to live free. We were being repressed because we were the Puerto Rican problem. There were too many Puerto Ricans: folks out in the street, cars driving around doing circles, honking horns, waving flags. The community out on their stoops. They're out celebrating.

There was no community policing engagement, where the cops approach people and want to be seen now with the photo ops and the propaganda where cops are in the parade, celebrating the community. Back then, it was just sweeping the street clean of Puerto Ricans. That was done violently by mandate by Giuliani. They ran people over, there was no conversation, it was just everyone being arrested.

We've documented young girls as young as eight being slammed by cops against storefront gates, their mothers protesting, being maced and attacked. They did this to the women, they did this to the children, and the young men caught beatings that traumatized generations. People's bones were broken, skulls were cracked, we bled. We shed blood for this. Our sweat and our blood and our pain was laid down as the sacrifice for what we have today. I'm getting goosebumps just remembering this, because it was painful.

It was unjust, to be ridiculed, to be humiliated, to be beaten and to be repressed. We created a way to defend ourselves through copwatching. It was nonviolent resistance, because it's a camera, we're holding up a mirror, we're documenting, and yes, it is a weapon. That weapon kept us safe. Although the police did all of that, it was evidence.

That collective resistance grew. Since the 90s and early 2000s, we began to lay the groundwork about what copwatch community resistance looks like. We would take over the corner on 49th Street and Fifth Avenue in Sunset Park. We brought over twenty or thirty copwatchers, but we would also bring bands that played traditional Afro-Puerto Rican folkloric music: bomba, plena. They would bring all their percussion and line up against the wall. We would not block pedestrian traffic. And we would film.

The cops would jump out of their cars, tell us to get the fuck out of there, and try to grab drums and attack us. But because there were so many cameras around, the community members felt safe to come around the space that we created.

When the cops came and threatened, some of the drummers were like: "Dennis, I can't get arrested for this, I got to go home." But there was an old woman that came and grabbed her percussion instrument. And she started playing her rhythm. She took the lead and she said, "Everybody, sit down and play now." All the drums got down and they started playing. And she held down the line when the cops were there watching; they were afraid of that woman, they were afraid of that elder because she held command. That was a just resistance.

This was cops being violent and repressive. And we were community members organized, fighting back. In front of the cameras, we documented ourselves saying to cops: there is pedestrian traffic that is not being obstructed. We don't need amplified sound, this is live percussion. We don't need sound permits, and we have a right to assemble. We're going to stay here and we're not moving.

And that group of 20 or 30 people turned into 500. We began to do this every year. Now the police show up with all their public relations and Community Affairs, and now they're like...our Puerto Rican problem became a *real* Puerto Rican problem.

We filed an application and created an official parade. For the last six years, prior to COVID, there has been a parade in Sunset Park created and founded by this resistance. It was created from community-led effort.

We're just like the St. Patrick's Day Parade, just like the Irish folks get to celebrate their day and cops don't fuck with them. Everybody out there gets to enjoy their beer, and finally we get to do the same. We all have a right. But it took resistance to force that to happen. Community brought about change.

JH: I want to circle back to something you said early on about how, when you started doing this, you didn't even know if it was allowed. Who were you able to connect with to learn what was okay?

DF: I was part of the Ñetas, which was a prisoners rights organization that, since the 1970s, fought for the rights of prisoners' to abolish prisons. I was in jail when I was a teenager. I didn't do more than a year, six months at Rikers Island. It was through there that I got involved with the Ñetas.

After being released from jail, me and a group of Ñetas were approached by former members of the Young Lords Party, Vicente "Panama" Alba and Richie Perez, who were founders of the National Congress for Puerto Rican rights. In the mid 90s, they were the backbone who helped organize the parents against police brutality. They have an organization, the National Congress for Puerto Rican rights, which organized parents whose children were murdered by the police in New York.

So the Ñetas, the Latin Kings, Zulu Nation, and all these street families were invited into the fold, to get us to work together. We were trying to transition from being a "gang" into being a revolutionary movement.

We were out there protesting against police brutality, organizing, doing security at protests, supporting parents, and that's where I began to document. It was there that I began to put words to what I'd been living, what I'd been experiencing. To understand what overpolicing of Black and Brown communities looked like. I began to learn to articulate it, and to define the mechanisms that we use to defend ourselves and protect ourselves.

This is something that I didn't invent. People all over the world instinctively began to film and document police. Instinctively, it's going to happen: people are going to resist and develop and evolve and figure out ways to survive.

JH: Looking back on all the work you've done with CopWatch over the last many decades, what really big accomplishments do you want other people to know about?

We needed to do this as a community, organized, because we are the only ones that are going to keep us safe.

DF: What brought about success was when we learned to do this collectively. We kept us safe: when we watch each other's backs, when we learn to survive this encounter. We need to be unified, we need to film each other filming the cops. That builds community and discipline. It takes away the "me, I" mentality. We needed to do this as a community, organized, because we are the only ones that are going to keep us safe.

As a tactic, to film each other filming the cops from various angles to cover the scene, with no blind spots, that tactic is what works. You could film cops and you might film something crazy and get famous and then become a target, like Ramsey Orta or the other woman who filmed Floyd's death. But police like to discredit the messenger; we can't do this alone. The community needs to support people who are doing this. And that's how we come out of this safe.

That's what I want folks to know: that we can succeed collectively. I think it's as simple as that.

JH: How has this work changed over the years, because of technology but also because of other factors that you've seen shift the way people do this work together?

DF: Technology has brought us to a place where we can turn the tables on powers that be, because we're equipped with this technology that is so easily accessible today. It has given all of us the power to be a citizen journalist, to document something and have that go viral. You can do that from behind your computer, behind your device. That is completely different. We can now catalog all of this footage and identify cops and create profiles, and put together incidents and document them. We have the power now to publish reports. The machine and the system only look at numbers; now we can spit their language back to them and force them to see what the public is documenting. That is a big step that we've taken in 20 years.

We need to create our own records, to track and connect the dots. The police don't provide information to the public, although they use public funds to keep these records. The public has no access, so we've developed this technology. Those are huge steps. That type of growth has come about because of consistency and dedication. There is community behind this. One individual can't make this happen. The more the people learn and develop and get involved, the more this strengthens.

JH: Looking forward, what are some of the big priorities that you have right now? What are other things that you really think the community needs to prioritize?

DF: Abolition is a process. We shouldn't lose focus of wanting to ultimately abolish the police and abolish the system. But let's not play into divisive politics, thinking that some of these reforms that a lot of folks are pushing for are misguided because they don't address policing as a whole in this country.

I'm not saying that there aren't nonprofits that make money off of reforming and having better training for police. But I think that we need to further define: what does abolition mean? What does that process look like? And how do we get there?

There's this call-out culture within abolition groups about campaigning to change laws, to take surveillance powers and drones away from the police— that this is reformist because it is looking through the courts and legislative process to try to disarm the police. I think there are so many different fronts on how we have to tackle this and how we have to abolish the cops. There are different parts of the body that are needed to fight. As a community, we need to define that and have these conversations in ways that we're not shooting ourselves in the foot.

We're not in a place where we can continue to allow COINTELPRO-type tactics to create divisions and shut down a movement, and make us inept and not able to fight. The powers that be have infiltrated for a very long time. They look for ways to divide and shut movements down. We need to get informed. We need to create a process for groups to communicate amongst themselves, to hold each other accountable in ways that are a part of restorative justice, but I'm not about shutting down groups and movements that need to exist to move this movement forward.

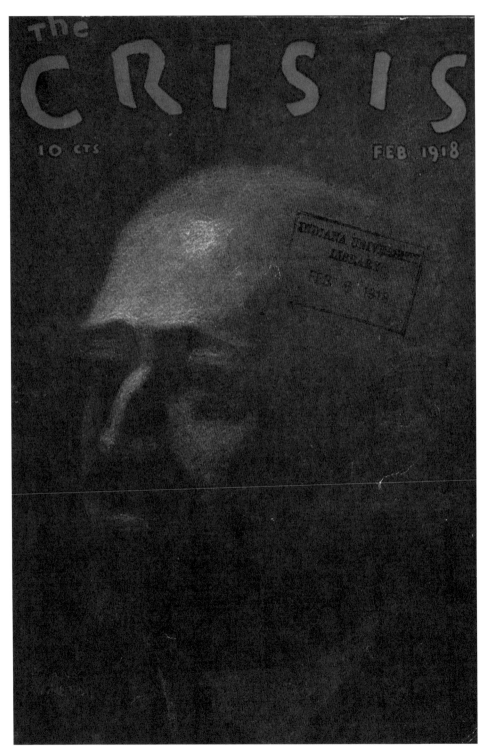

The Crisis, February 1918, cover art by Frank Walts.

EYES ON THE STATE

Every struggle requires many tactics; resistance against police violence includes observation, record keeping, communication about injustices perpetrated, direct intervention, as well as attempts to change the laws, funding, and structure of the police. In the early 20th century, W.E.B. Du Bois's publication *The Crisis: A Record of the Darker Races* began recording eye-witness accounts of lynchings in the United States and acts of police brutality or white violence. *The Crisis* reported violence that the white press would not document or condemn. Black weeklies like *The New York Amsterdam News* and *The People's Voice* in Harlem also regularly covered police violence. The legacy of documenting what the mainstream press and law enforcement agencies themselves would not report continued during the explosion of Leftist press in the 1960s and 1970s, with underground newspapers like *The Black Panther, LA Free Press, Palante,* and many more. The Marxist-Leninist League of Revolutionary Black Workers in Detroit published lists of Black people murdered by police in their newspaper *The Inner City Voice.* As technologies changed, groups like CopWatch continued the legacy of the Black Panthers and Young Lords while using handheld cameras and later cell phones to record encounters with the police.

CopWatch

CopWatch was developed in 1990 in response to police violence and surveillance in homeless encampments in Berkeley, California. After the Berkeley chapter was established, the tactic quickly spread to a dozen cities across the US. These groups all share the core tactic of organizing citizens to document police engagements with the community (often during both traffic stops and arrests). Because CopWatch is not a formal, centralized entity, but instead a tactic that can be used by anyone, hundreds of local chapters across the country have been set up over the past thirty years. Groups often develop and are extremely active after high profile policing abuses, some only lasting a year or two, others for decades. The work of CopWatch was initially done with handheld video cameras, with footage often shared with the media or families and legal teams of those victimized by the police. Now, with the ability to stream from a cell phone camera directly to social media, organized groups are less visible—although they still exist—and the tactic is in common use amongst the broader public.

Dennis Flores reflects on the evolution of his own work with CopWatch tactics in New York City:

"I was 19 or 20 years old, born and raised in Sunset Park, and like many young people of color, heavily targeted by the police. As soon as I left my stoop or went to a park to meet friends there was always an encounter with the cops, on a daily basis.

Those engagements meant cops rushing us from their cars as we're hanging out. You would have this attack of cops charging you, tackling you, slamming you to the floor, and arresting you. I had no words to explain what the hell was happening to me and my peers, other than knowing instinctively that I needed to document it. I was bold enough to document cops as they approached us in this manner, photographing or tape recording them, being arrested for it dozens of times, but it became clear that this is a tactic that is keeping me safe. This is a weapon. Now, when the cops jumped at us from their cars, I dared take that bold stance and record them and hold up a tape recorder and start taking photos. That began to set a precedent and send the message. I got pounced on, beat up, or thrown in jail. But time and time again, being consistent, continuing to do this, beginning to organize

People's Justice for Community Control & Police Accountability, *Staten Island It's Time For Us All To Watch the Cops!* (Staten Island, NY), flier, 2014.

N. A. A. C. P. — 183

be given a "decent lynching," and that they consider the burning and torturing a disgrace to the community. By this it meant a quick, quiet hanging, with no display or torturing.

The identity of the mob leaders is known all over Dyer County. From all accounts, they are citizens of doubtful reputation, backed up for this occasion by the sentiment of the community at large.

A prosperous citizen made the remark that these men were no better than the Negro. He was threatened at once with lynching. This remark has, however, been made by others, as well as by the man threatened.

Street talk in Dyersburg on Monday had not yet been touched by reflection. One man, who had been out of town on Sunday, was heard to say with gusto: "The best part about it was the burning. This hanging kills too quick. If I'd been here I'd have helped."

Another commented: "It was the biggest thing since Ringling Brothers' Circus came to town."

A few people—mostly women—said: "It was terrible."

Many citizens seem to have the psychology of having performed an unpleasant duty. One citizen said: "People here can do a thing like that, and then forget all about it."

LYNCHINGS AND MOB MURDERS, 1917

ACCORDING to the Crisis records there were 224 persons lynched and killed by mob violence in the United States during the year 1917. Of these 46 were lynchings of persons accused of crime and misdemeanors. The record of the Negroes killed follows:

Proctor, Ark., February 9—James Smith (alias Coy Anderson), hanged; murder.
Hammond, La., February 28—Emma Hooper, hanged; wounding a constable.
Meigs, Ga., March 2—Linton Clinton, shot; assault upon a white girl.
Maysville, Ky., March 12—William Sanders, hanged; robbery.
Dyersburg, Tenn., March 19—William Thomas, hanged; shooting an officer.
Kissimmee, Fla., March 27—S. C. Garner, hanged; refusal to give up farm.
Pelham, Ga., March 28—Joe Nowling, hanged; reason unknown.

Shreveport, La., May 11—Henry Brooks, shot; intimacy with a white woman.
Fulton, Ky., May 20—Lawrence Dempsey, hanged; wounding a railroad watchman.
Memphis, Tenn., May 22—Ell Persons, burned; rape and murder.
Columbia, Miss., June 2—Van Hayes, hanged; murder.
Holdenville, Okla., June 16—Henry Conley, hanged; assault upon a white woman.
Courtney, Tex., June 21—Ben Harper, hanged; he drove an automobile that ran down and killed a white girl.
Riesel, Tex., June 23—Elijah Hays, beaten to death; striking a white woman.
Cleveland, Fla., June 24—Shep Trent, shot; attempt to attack a white woman.
Galveston, Tex., June 25—Chester Sawyer, hanged; attacking a white woman.
Temple, Tex., June 29—Robert Jefferson, shot; without provocation.
East St. Louis, Ill., July 2—175 colored men, women, and children slain by mobs.
Orange, Tex., July 3—Gilbert Guidry, hanged; charged with attempted rape.
Edgard, La., July 16—Marcel Ruffin, drowned; vagrancy.
Reform, Ala., July 16—Unidentified Negro, hanged; petty theft.
Pickens County, Ala., July 23—Poe Hibbler, hanged; attempted assault upon a white girl.
Elysian Fields, Tex., July 23—Unnamed, hanged; entering a woman's room.
Letchatchie, Ala., July 25—Will Powell and Jesse Powell, hanged; insolence.
Amite, La., July 30—Dan Rout and Jerry Rout, hanged; murder.
Garland City, Okla., July 31—Arland Avery, hanged; robbery.
Ashdown, Ark., August 9—Aaron Jimerson, hanged; attacking a constable.
Heathsville, Va., August 16—William Page, hanged; attempted assault upon a white girl.
Memphis, Tenn., August 17—Strickland, hanged; reason unknown.
Marshall, Tex., August 22—Charles Jones, hanged; entering room of a white woman.
York, S. C., August 23—W. T. Sims, shot; opposing draft law.
Chester, Pa., Sept. 3—3 colored men killed by mob.

184 — THE CRISIS

Beaumont, Tex., Sept. 5—Charles Jennings, shot; cause unknown.
Athens, Ga., Sept. 18—Rufus Moncrief, hanged; attacking a white woman.
Goose Creek, Tex., Sept. 21—Bert Smith, hanged; attacking a white woman.
England, Ark., Sept. 21—Sam Cates, shot; annoying white girls.
Danville, Va., October 12—Walter Clark, shot; resisting arrest.
New Orleans, La.—Fred Johnson, hanged; robbery.
Quitman, Ga., Nov. 10—Jesse Staten, shot; insolent letter to a white woman.
Sale City, Ga., Nov. 17—Collins Johnson and D. C. Johnson, hanged; disputing white man's word.
Welch, W. Va., Nov. 22—Unidentified Negro, shot; attacking white women.
Dyersburg, Tenn., Dec. 2—Ligon Scott, burned; attacking a white woman.
Rock Springs, Wyo., Dec. 14—Wade Hampton, hanged; annoying white women.
Matter, Ga., Dec. 15—Clinton Dekle, hanged; killing in quarrel.

LYNCHINGS AND MOB MURDERS OF NEGROES BY STATES

Illinois	175
Texas	9
Alabama	3
Louisiana	6
Georgia	7
Arkansas	3
Tennessee	4
Oklahoma	2
Pennsylvania	3
Florida	2
Kentucky	2
Mississippi	1
West Virginia	1
South Carolina	1
Virginia	1
Wyoming	1
Total	**222**

LYNCHINGS BY RACE

Negro	44
White	2

LYNCHINGS AND MOB MURDERS OF NEGROES BY ALLEGED CRIMES

Rape and attempted rape	11
Murder	5
Assault and wounding	4
Robbery and theft	6
White women (intimacy, annoying, striking, entering), etc.	7
Race prejudice (refusing to give up farm, accidental killing)	2
Opposing draft	1
Resisting arrest	1
Unreported	4
Vagrancy, disputing	3
Killed by mobs	178
Total	**222**

COLORED MEN LYNCHED BY YEARS 1885-1917

Year	No.	Year	No.
1885	78	1903	86
1886	71	1904	83
1887	80	1905	61
1888	95	1906	64
1889	95	1907	60
1890	90	1908	97
1891	121	1909	73
1892	155	1910	65
1893	154	1911	63
1894	134	1912	63
1895	112	1913	79
1896	80	1914	69
1897	122	1915	80
1898	102	1916	54
1899	84	1917	44
1900	107		
1901	107		
1902	86	**Total**	**2,911**

TO THE UNITED STATES OF NORTH AMERICA

By THOMAS CAMPBELL—1777-1834

UNITED STATES, your banner wears
Two emblems—one of fame;
Also, the other that it bears
Reminds us of your shame.

Your standard's constellation types
White freedom by its stars;
But what's the meaning of the stripes?
They mean your Negroes' scars.

"Lynchings and Mob Murders 1917," *The Crisis*, February 1918, pp. 183-184.

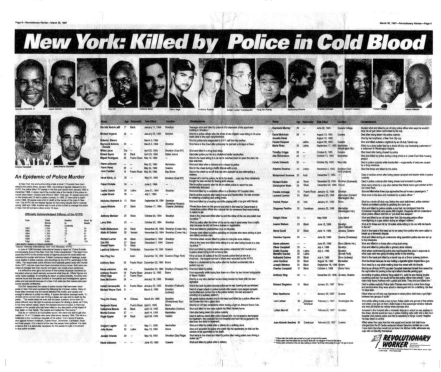

Revolutionary Worker, *New York: Killed by Police in Cold Blood* (New York, NY), newspaper, 1997, pp. 8-9.

myself and my friends to do this, that was a deterrent for the police.

The Puerto Rican Day Parade, since I can remember in the late 90s, is a huge parade. After the parade ended in the early evening, our community gathered and were met with overpolicing of our neighborhood; they would bring in cops from all the precincts around to clean out the neighborhood. Clean out means: no Puerto Ricans in the street. There was no community policing engagement, where the cops approach people and want to be seen now with the photo ops and the propaganda that where cops are in the parade, celebrating the community. Back then, it was just sweeping

the street clean of Puerto Ricans. That was done violently by mandate by Giuliani. We've documented young girls as young as eight being slammed by cops against storefront gates, their mothers protesting, being maced and attacked. They did this to the women, they did this to the children, and the young men caught beatings that traumatized generations."

"We created a way to defend ourselves through CopWatch. It was nonviolent resistance, because it's a camera, we're holding up a mirror, we're documenting, and yes, it is a weapon. That weapon kept us safe."

IF THE POLICE ARREST YOU...

•You may be handcuffed, searched, photographed and fingerprinted.

•Say repeatedly, "I DON'T WANT TO TALK UNTIL MY LAWYER IS PRESENT." Even if your rights aren't read, refuse to talk until your lawyer/public defender arrives.

•Do not talk to inmates in jail about your case.

•If you're on probation/parole, tell your P.O. you've been arrested, but NOTHING ELSE.

Police can arrest someone they believe is "interfering" with their actions. Maintain a reasonable distance, and if cops threaten to arrest you, EXPLAIN THAT YOU DON'T INTEND TO INTERFERE, BUT YOU HAVE THE RIGHT TO OBSERVE THEIR ACTIONS.

REMEMBER
You have legal rights, but many police will not respect your rights
BE CAREFUL – BE STREET SMART

IMPORTANT PHONE NUMBERS:
National Lawyers Guild - SF
Demonstration line ... (415) 285-1011
NorCal ACLU .... (415) 621-2488

IN BERKELEY:
CopWatch ....(510) 548-0425
Public Defender ....(510) 268-7400
UC Jail ....(510) 642-6760
Jail ....(510) 981-5766
Police Review
Commission ....(510) 981-4950

IN OAKLAND:
Jail .... (510) 238-3575
Public Defender ...... (510) 268-7400
Citizens' PRB .... (510) 238-3159
Critical Resistance .. (510) 444-0484
PUEBLO ....(510) 535-2525

COPWATCH
POCKET GUIDE

2022 Blake Street
Berkeley, CA 94704
(510) 548-0425
www.berkeleycopwatch.org

YOU HAVE THE RIGHT...

•to be in a public place and to observe police activity.

IF THE POLICE STOP ANYONE...

•STOP AND WATCH.

•Write down officers' names, badge numbers, and car numbers. COPS MUST BE IDENTIFIED BY NAME OR BADGE NUMBER *(PC sec. 830.10).*

•Write down the time, date, and place of the incident and all details as soon as possible.

•Ask if the person is being arrested, and if so, on what charge.

•Get witnesses' names and contact info.

•Try to get the arrestee's name, but only if they already gave it to the police.

•Document any injuries as soon as possible. Photograph them and have a medical report describing details of the injuries.

IF THE POLICE STOP YOU...

•Ask, "AM I FREE TO GO?" If not, you are being detained. If yes, walk away.

•Ask, "WHY ARE YOU DETAINING ME?" To stop you, the officer must have a "reasonable suspicion" to suspect your involvement in a specific crime *(not just a guess or a stereotype).*

•It is not a crime to be without ID. If you are being detained or issued a ticket, you may want to show ID to the cop because they can take you to the station to verify your identity.

•If a cop tries to search your car, your house, or your person say repeatedly that you DO NOT CONSENT TO THE SEARCH. If in a car, do not open your trunk or door – by doing so you consent to a search of your property and of yourself. If at home, step outside and lock your door behind you so cops have

no reason to enter your house. Ask to see the warrant and check for proper address, judge's signature, and what the warrant says the cops are searching for. Everything must be correct in a legal warrant. Otherwise, send the police away.

•The cops can do a "pat search" (search the exterior of one's clothing for weapons) during a detention for "officer safety reasons". They can't go into your pockets or bags without your consent. If you are arrested, they can search you and your possessions in great detail.

•DO NOT RESIST PHYSICALLY. Use your words and keep your cool. If an officer violates your rights, don't let them provoke you into striking back. Wait until you are out of custody then you can organize for justice.

CopWatch,
CopWatch Pocket Guide (Berkeley, CA), brochure, n.d.

2018.009

KNOW YOUR RIGHTS
WATCH THE COPS!

COPWATCH is a community self-defense tactic.

COPWATCH teams of community members legally observe and document POLICE ACTIVITY using video cameras.

KNOW YOUR RIGHTS NYC COPWATCH
4 TIPS TO PROTECT YOURSELF:

You have the right to watch and film police activities.

If you are harassed by the police, write down the officer's badge, car number, name and/or other identifying information. **Get medical attention if you** need it and take pictures of any injuries.

If you are detained or arrested by a police officer, demand to speak with an attorney and don't tell them anything until an attorney is present.

You do not have to consent to a search of yourself, your car or your house. Do NOT try to physically stop the police. Simply say you do not consent to the search out loud.

Contact us if you would like a **Know Your Rights** training or to learn how to create a **CopWatch** Team in your community.

produced by

PEOPLES' JUSTICE
for Community Control & Police Accountability

PO Box 1885 NY NY 10159
www.Peoplesjustice.org
212-614-5343

CopWatch / People's Justice for Community Control & Police Accountability, *Know Your Rights Watch the Cops!* (New York, NY), flier, 2014.

Stolen Lives Project

The Stolen Lives Project, established in 1996, was the first attempt to create a comprehensive list of those murdered by police or those who have died in police custody within the US. Prior to this, the Federal Department of Justice was documenting and reporting a fraction of annual killings at the hands of police, citing a lack of funding to document incidents. A joint project of the National Lawyers Guild, the October 22nd Coalition, and the Anthony Baez Foundation, the Stolen Lives Project published multiple editions of a book documenting these killings, the most recent in 1999. In the 2000s, the organization created a series of online updates, but eventually the level of attention placed on police killings led to more mainstream tracking projects, including

Anthony Baez Foundation Staff, National Lawyers Guild Staff, October 22 Coalition to Stop Police Brutality Staff, *Stolen Lives: Killed by Law Enforcement* (New York: October Twenty-Second Coalition), 1999.

those maintained today by *The Washington Post* and *The Guardian*.

The October 22nd Coalition (full name: October 22nd Coalition to Stop Police Brutality, Repression and the Criminalization of a Generation) was the activist element of the Stolen Lives Project. A national umbrella organization with different participants in different cities, the main organizing body of the coalition was the Revolutionary Communist Party. It was initially convened in 1996 when the group called for a national day of protest against police brutality (on October 22nd), involving many family members of those killed by the police. In the late 1990s and early 2000s, it created spin-off projects such as Against the Nightstick, a series of art exhibitions drawing attention to the issue.

Families of victims have often been at the forefront of organizing for justice and reform. After Amadou Diallo's shooting in 1999 by a group of plainclothes officers in New York City, the NYPD defunded and eventually disbanded the Street Crime Unit these officers had been part of. Tyisha Miller's murder by police officers in Riverside, California in 1998 instigated an investigation by the Federal Department of Justice and the United States Attorney's office into civil rights violations by the Riverside Police Department, and the police killings of LaTanya Haggerty, Rekia Boyd, Shantel Davis, Alberta Spruill, Kendra James, Shelly Frey, Kayla Moore, Kyam Livingston, Miriam Carey, Michelle Cusseaux, Tanisha Anderson and more have been memorialized by their families and by the #SayHerName movement,

October 22 Coalition, *Against the Nightstick: Art Against Police Brutality* (Chicago, IL), flier, 1999.

which highlights the crisis of Black women and girls targeted by police violence. #SayHerName began with a social media campaign in 2015 and a report on the specific gendered violence experienced by Black women, girls, and femmes published by the African American Policy Forum and in response to the absence of Black female victims in the media coverage of #BlackLivesMatter. Executive Director Kimberlé Crenshaw said, "If you say the name, you're prompted to learn the story, and if you know the story, then you have a broader sense of all the ways Black bodies are made vulnerable to police violence." The #SayHerName Mothers Network has held annual vigils, campaigned in Washington, and attended the 2017 Women's March on Washington.

Dread Scott, an artist who organized with the October 22nd Coalition, reflects on the role of family members coming together in response to their loved ones' deaths at the hands of police:

"The epidemic of police killing, I think, has been a constant feature of America. But it was these few courageous parents—who were isolated in many ways in the late 80s and early 90s—that first came together. It was mostly Latinas in the Bronx like Margarita Rosario and Iris Baez, and Nicholas Heyward, Sr. in Brooklyn. Now, there is a sort of a righteousness that is associated with parents standing up to murder by police. But then, it was almost like the radical shift that Mamie Till made when she said, "No, I'm going to display my son's body. This is what you did." And calling on Black people to say, "Let's not suffer in silence, we're going to stand up." Anthony Baez was killed because his fucking football hit a cop car. They choked him to death. And Anthony Rosario and Hilton Vega were shot in the back. They were executed by cops who would become Giuliani's bodyguards, while lying face down in an apartment in the Bronx."

Dread Scott, *Danger: Police in Area* (New York, NY), street sign, 1999/2000.

Artist Dread Scott created and reproduced this sign after the 1999 murder of 23-year-old Amadou Diallo. Diallo was shot 41 times by plainclothes officers from NYPD's Street Crime Unit who stopped Diallo outside of his apartment and began shooting when he reached for his wallet.

Copaganda

The Black press played a major role in pushing back on one of the most pernicious tools the police have in swaying public opinion: copaganda. In addition to films and television shows that portray the police as doggedly fighting crime and competently solving murders, the mainstream press perpetuates the image of police that serve the public. Mainstream press historically and currently takes official police statements as fact and has stoked fears of rising crime rates while continually characterizing

Black Americans, and in particular Black youth, as criminals. As more Black workers moved to the industrialized Northern cities in the 1940s, newspapers published racist accounts of crimes perpetrated on white victims. *The Crisis* called out *The New York Times* in 1941 for manufacturing "a 'crime wave' in Harlem," and wrote that the *Times* had, "by persistent distortion and misrepresentation... branded the 200,000 residents of that section as criminals."

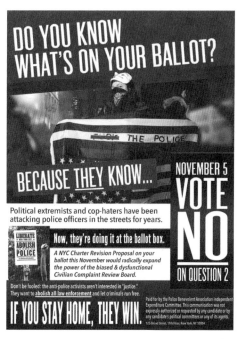

NYPD, *Welcome to Fear City*, (New York, NY) 1975. The NYPD created and distributed this infamous pamphlet in 1975 to tourists arriving at New York airports.

Do you know what's on your ballot? Police Benevolent Association Independent Expenditure Committee (New York, NY), 2019.

This ad appeared in local papers in October 2019, urging the public to vote "NO" on the attempt to strengthen the powers of the CCRB.

Jargon used and invented by police often sneaks its way into mainstream press and normalizes and obscures the violence of the police. The phrase "officer-involved shooting" was first created by the LAPD in the early 1970s and the Department even had a position called the "supervisor of the Officer-Involved-Shooting Section." The media routinely uses this type of passive voice when simply stating that "police shot and killed a person" would be more precise.

But the most stubborn myth perpetuated by the police is that they have a monopoly on public safety and crime prevention. The police claim to be the "Thin Blue Line" that stands between ordinary citizens and criminals and that they are the last guard against violence and political radicalism. The phrase "Thin Blue Line" itself evokes soldiers keeping combatants at bay, and police use this war-like imagery whenever they are met with resistance or reform, and whenever their power and budget is threatened.

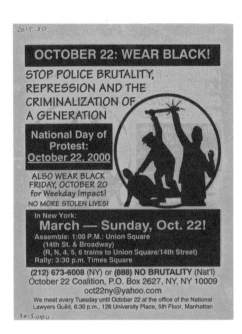

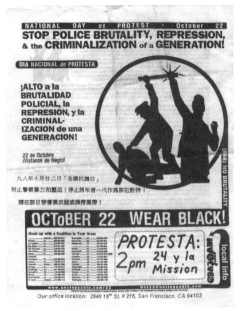

October 22 Coalition, *Stop Police Brutality, Repression and the Criminalization of a Generation* (New York, NY), poster, 2000.

October 22 Coalition, *Stop Police Brutality, Repression & the Criminalization of a Generation* (San Francisco, CA), poster, 1998.

October 22 Coalition, *National March to Stop Police Terror* (New York, NY), flier, 2014/2015.

HOW PIGS KILL-101

1. Police kill unarmed citizen.

2. a. Nobody cares (end lesson)

   b. Public outrage (continue to #3)

3. Faux investigation **OF** the pigs,

   BY the pigs.

4. Wait for public sentiment to die down.

5. Announce that officer _(name here)_

   was justified in

   the use of

   lethal

   force.

   (repeat)   Kendra James   May 5, 2003

How Pigs Kill-101, (Portland, OR), sticker, 2003.

Dread Scott

Interviewed by JOSH MACPHEE

Dread Scott is a visual artist who focuses on making revolutionary art to propel history forward. His work highlighting brutality has included involvement with the October 22 Coalition to Stop Police Brutality, Repression and the Criminalization of a Generation, and with their Against the Nightstick project.

JOSH MACPHEE: At Interference Archive, we're working on a project about the history of organizing against police violence. What can you tell us about this work, and what was your involvement in it?

DREAD SCOTT: I recall a kind of progression. There was an organization called Parents Against Police Brutality; key people in that included Margarita Rosario and Iris Baez. Refuse & Resist was probably doing work at that time, but the parents really came together.

Some supporters, including the RCP (Revolutionary Communist Party), were talking with them and working to create an organization of family members. Now, there are lots of family organizations, with very, very high profile resistance to police killings: families of Oscar Grant, of George Floyd, of Tamir Rice. But in the late 80s and early 90s, there were only a couple: some Latinas the Bronx, who very quickly connected to Nicholas Hayward, whose son was killed in Brooklyn in '94. Through that, as it appeared to me, the October 22nd Coalition was forged.

As an artist, I and some others started doing things around that, but it was these few courageous parents—who were isolated in many ways in the late 80s and early 90s—that first came together. Now there is a sort of a righteousness that is associated with parents standing up to murder by police. But then, it was almost like the radical shift that Mamie Till made when she said, "No, I'm going to display my son's body. This is what you did." And calling on Black people to say, "Let's not suffer in silence, we're going to stand up." Anthony Baez was killed because his fucking football hit a cop car. They choked him to death. And Anthony Rosario and Hilton Vega were shot in the back. They were executed while lying face down in an apartment in the Bronx, by cops who would become Giuliani's bodyguards.

JM: October 22 was nominally a coalition, right?

DS: Yeah. It really was. I don't remember how it got started. And then Stolen Lives Project, which was an offshoot of that, started with the National Lawyers Guild to crowdsource an accounting of all the people killed by police. Initially it was just a saddle-stitch book that probably had about 1,000 people documented in the 90s who were killed by the police. And then after that, there was a perfect bound book that came out.

Now there is a sort of righteousness that is associated with parents standing up to murder by police. But then, it was almost like the radical shift that Mamie Till made when she said, "No, I'm going to display my son's body. This is what you did."

That was the first attempt at a national accounting of the people killed by police. And it was activist, grassroots organizations that did it. I think the Stolen Lives book probably had about 2000 people that were killed in a decade. And now *The Washington Post* and *The Guardian* have taken it up; *The Guardian* comes in and has many more resources (including the Internet), and then it's like, oh, wait, police killed 1,100 people a year. And so that first accounting was off by a factor of five, but it was a first accounting.

There was a demonstration that happened probably about 1998 or '99. This demonstration had signs of people's names. This was a project that I initiated, working with Brad McCallum and Jenny Polak, where we made square posters that had eyes of people and said "killed by police," and had a person's name. The demonstration started in Union Square, with all these images recognizing and honoring all the names of people that were killed. Most of the people were Black or Brown, but there were names of Asians that were killed or names of white people that were killed. And it was an interesting thing, marching down Broadway, to have recognition of all these names, made possible by the Stolen Lives Project.

We got a set of PSAs made about police brutality that got on MTV. Wyclef was in the first one; it was this question of art and activism merging. We were able to go to a concert, Wyclef had dropped *Carnival*, and we told him, "There are these family members who are standing up against police brutality; there's this national day of police brutality; you should make a PSA." The production values, the logo and infographics, were not great, but it was like activists busted onto MTV. It was under the auspices of the October 22nd Coalition, with a filmmaker named David Lindblom; his day gig was as an editor at some TV station or something like that. Now everybody can do video on their phone but back then, doing decent video was hard. He had access to camera equipment and editing facilities and stuff, and so we shot a broadcast-quality video.

It was mostly him and me working on that, with a crew that was a little larger. Some of the people would ultimately go on to be part of the artist network of Refuse & Resist, but at the time, it was just a loose conglomeration of people who were doing something for the October 22nd day of protest. We weren't really a group, we were just people who knew each other.

JM: Partly because of the architecture of the internet, the 60s, 70s, and even
the 80s are pretty well documented, but there's all this stuff that happened
in the 90s and early 2000s that just isn't online. It's just as if no one even
acknowledges it exists. I think that makes it really important to get these
stories out there and show that there's a continuous history.

DS: For better or worse, my generation tried valiantly but we failed hard. The gulf
between 1969 and 2016 is pretty vast. It's not that nothing happened in
that period. But politically, on a lot of different fronts, it's not a good period.
In May and June (of 2020), and even some of the precursors leading up to
what is broadly defined as Black Lives Matter, but also stuff going on with
the Extinction Rebellion and #MeToo, the resistance and organization and
some of the theoretical frameworks that people are developing are much
better than anything in the 80s and 90s. That's unfortunate, but I think it's
just true. It's not just: why didn't those of us who were in our 30s in the 90s,
why didn't we just do better? If you're writing a broad art history of the past
100 years of struggle, you could kind of skip the 90s.

I think there's a lot to learn from. But I'm more interested in what younger
people today are doing, and how things are being organized. I wish some of
them would learn more from us older people, in a certain sense, because I
do see a bit of reinvention of the wheel and making the same mistakes. But I
also think: there's a lot you guys have got right.

JM: In 1998-99, I got involved in the Against the Nightstick stuff in Chicago. It
was never clear to me whether that was a Chicago-specific project or whether
there was Against the Nightstick in other cities.

DS: I think LA did one too but I think it was really in Chicago. I sent out some
artwork to one of the editions of it, and I was really happy that it happened.
Do you know Dave Thorne? He was doing these poster projects. I think one
of them was specifically focused on police brutality; some of it he was doing
with Refuse & Resist, and some of it he was doing as Resistant Strains. I
think that he either contributed a set of posters to Against the Nightstick
or maybe had a showing wherever he was, which was, I think, someplace
in Vermont. So, I think that Against the Nightstick started in Chicago, but
inspired a couple other things.

JM: I know that at some point, I think in the later 90s, you did those big yellow signs. Can you share the story around that?

DS: Amadou Diallo was killed in '99, and I just quickly made a sketch of "Danger: Police in Area." I thought it should be a print, and at that point I hadn't done any screenprinting. I had some friends, and we said, let's figure this out. I think one of them had gone to Pratt and maybe had access to some facilities. We made screens, and we did some printing; the initial prints weren't great, because we were not master printers. We were more like, you know, street artists, and we thought: it's good enough. We posted some of those around, and it was really cool.

And then I got invited to what became a 2001 residency at the Lower East Side Printshop. I did a suite of prints, and that was one of the prints I did. It got printed as a fine art edition where the printing quality was better, and then also on metal. So the concept was from '99, I think the first printing happened in '99, and then we did good prints in 2001. And then I just gave the art to various activist communities and made T-shirts. At one point, I saw documentation of a demonstration in LA where there were hundreds, literally hundreds of people who had this T-shirt. I think the artists network of Refuse & Resist probably produced them. And then I gave the art to Revolution Books in New York, and I think they got it out to LA, but there were literally thousands of shirts made.

It really stemmed from the police killing of Amadou Diallo, who was an African immigrant who was shot in his doorway by undercover cops. In all likelihood he thought they were coming to rob him, so he reached to hand his wallet to them, and they murdered him in a hail of 41 bullets. That was the first highly visible police killing that generated resistance in my adult lifetime. Before that, there were Michael Stewart and Eleanor Bumpurs, but they were before I got to New York and even those weren't as high profile. Those had kind of gotten confined to activists. With Amadou Diallo, it was literally front page news. It became a Bruce Springsteen song. It turned a corner, and so when this artwork came out, it really captured a lot of people's imaginations, which was great.

One thing I will say about the metal sign is, I intended to put them up in locations where the police had killed somebody. I printed the work in spring or early summer of 2001, and then the World Trade Center attack happened and resistance had to change. There were profound questions of what people do in the face of US imperialism, and the tremendous repression that existed against Muslims; overnight, people were just disappeared. People that were not disappeared had to prove their loyalty to America, and so the movement against police brutality kind of got pushed into the background in a weird way, even though the police still were clearly brutalizing people, including a lot of Muslims and Arabs, but it took a different context.

And so, I didn't post up any of the metal signs until 2002 or 2003. I lived in Fort Greene, which is a largely upper middle class neighborhood, but it borders a housing project, the Walt Whitman Houses. I woke up to gunshots; hearing gunshots in New York is not that out of place, but there were a lot of them. I thought: the police have probably killed somebody. I woke up in the morning, and I saw on the news that they had killed Floyd Quinones. I didn't know him, but I walked to where he was killed. People were grieving; he was very loved in that community. And I said: I've got this sign, would it be okay if we put one up? And they were like, that'd be great. We put one up, and it was a real lockdown situation in the neighborhood at the time. The police were really, really going crazy; they brought in trucks, and they closed off roads. They also went into the projects and started messing with people. The police were issuing warrants for misdemeanors that were a decade or more old; they were just screwing with people. And so in that context, literally under the noses of the cops, we put up the sign. They were really pissed. But it stayed up for eight hours and the people there really, really loved it.

Dread Scott, *Danger: Police in Area* (New York, NY), street sign, 1999/2000.

The Black Panther, Vol 11 No 1 (Oakland, CA), newspaper, 1968. Illustration by Emory Douglas.

NAMING THE PROBLEM: PIG NATION

While there is evidence that the police have been called "pigs" going back to the early 19th century, the leap from a marginal term to one taken up by masses of protesters happened in the late 1960s and was most creatively popularized by Emory Douglas, the Minister of Propaganda for the Black Panther Party. His comic illustrations of police as pigs were featured in almost every issue of *The Black Panther* newspaper throughout the late 1960s and 1970s. These cartoons were picked up and repurposed by many other groups,

featured in other underground newspapers, and used on fliers and posters.

The Young Lords also featured a "Pig of the Week" in their newspaper, *Palante*, highlighting, among others, the violence of Philadelphia police commissioner Frank Rizzo, national president of the Fraternal Order of Police John Harrington, and Patrolmen's Benevolent Association president Edward J. Kiernan.

Oink Stay In Line (New York, NY), sticker, n.d.

Emory Douglas, "All Power to the People." *The Black Panther*, newspaper, October 18, 1969.

(Clockwise from top-left) Emory Douglas, "We want an end to the robbery by the capitalists of our Black community," *The Black Panther*, (Oakland, CA), newspaper.

Emory Douglas, "U.S. Imperialism, Black Capitalism," *The Black Panther*, (Oakland, CA) newspaper, March 16, 1969.

"Pig of the Week," *Palante Vol 2 No 10* (New York, NY), newspaper, August 28, 1970.

Emory Douglas, "It's All The Same," *The Black Panther* (Oakland, CA), newspaper, March 16, 1968.

Palante   Page 11

PIG
OF THE
WEEK

When Philadelphia police commissioner frank rizzo said, "We have to use force just like any army does. It's war, but I don't think we'll ever need federal troops. We're becoming familiar with guerrilla tactics, and we have the weapons to fight a war. I consider myself an expert in guerrilla warfare and I don't know of any problem we can't handle. We may have a riot here, but it will be the shortest riot in history.....''—when he said this he was telling the Puerto Rican and Black people of Philadelphia that if they ever took to the streets to complain about another brother or sister being killed by rizzo's murdering police force or any one of the thousand illegal acts amerikkkan oppressors commit against our people, that he, frank rizzo, could and would stop them—no matter how many of us he has to kill in order to do it.

To back up this boast he brags about his 125 man "S Force" that just drives around looking for trouble; or, as he says, "hunting teams, turned loose to hunt." Each "S" car carries: 2 M-70 Winchester rifles with scopes, 2 M-12 Winchester Shotguns-12 gauge, 1 .45 caliber Thompson submachine gun, 1 M-1 carbine, 1 tear gas gun, with hundreds of rounds for each. Back at the pig sty he has a .50 caliber machine gun that fires a special bullet that explodes when it hits walls.

frank rizzo, you are a lunatic intent on committing genocide. You aren't just an unknowing lackey of amerikkkan racism and oppression. You are a willing accomplice in the plot to exterminate our people. You have made plans for the slaughter of Puerto Rican and Black people by the hundreds. Bullets that explode when they hit walls also explode when they hit the heads of innocent children.

The day is drawing near, frank rizzo, when you will face the people's justice, and no number of tanks and airplanes can equal the power of the people. When they come to execute the sentence, when that day comes, remember——you said it was war!

THE WILL OF THE PEOPLE IS STRONGER THAN ALL OF THE MAN'S WEAPONS!

Luis A. Perez
Finance Ministry
YOUNG LORDS PARTY
Bronx Branch

EL PUERCO DE LA SEMANA

Cuando el comisario de policía de Philadelphia, frank rizzo, dijo, "Tenemos que usar la fuerza como lo hace cualquier otro ejército. Esto es guerra, pero dudo que necesitaremos las tropas federales. Nos estamos familiarizando con las tácticas de guerrilla y tenemos las armas para pelear una guerra. Me considero un experto en la guerra y dudo que haya problema que no podamos resolver. Quizás tendremos una rebelión aquí, pero será la rebelión mas insignificante en la historia de las rebeliones..." le estaba diciendo a los pueblos Puertorriqueños y Negros de Philadelphia que si algun dia se apoderaban de las calles para quejarse de la muerte de otro hermano o hermana por los puercos de rizzo—en cualquiera de las miles de razones illegales que usan los opresores en contra de nuestra gente—que él mismo, frank rizzo, podía y si los pararía, no importar le cuantas de nuestra vidas le costaría para hacer esto.

Para afirmar esto el dijo que tiene una "Fuerza S" de 125 hombres que solamente pasean en automobil en las comunidades buscando revolú, o como dice el puerco rizzo, "equipos de casería sueltos para cazar." Cada carro carga con: 2 rifles M-70 Winchester con alcances, 2 escopetas M-12 Winchester-12 ga., 1 sub-ametralladora .45 cal. Thompson, 1 carabina M-1, 1 revolver de gas lacrimógeno, con cien cargas de municiones para cada uno. Mientras en su corral de puercos tiene una ametralladora que dispara una descarga especial que explota cuando hace contacto con una pared.

frank rizzo, tu eres un maniático resuelto a cometer genocidio. No eres solamente un monigote ignorante de los opresores amerikkkanos. Tu eres un complice deseoso en el plan de exterminar a nuestra gente. Tu has trazado los planes para la matanza de la gente Puertorriqueña y Negra por los cientos. Balas que explotan cuando chocan con paredes, también explotan cuando chocan en contra de las cabezas de niños inocentes.

El día se esta acercando, frank rizzo, cuando te tendrás que confrontar con la justicia de la gente, y ningún número de tanques y aeroplanos podrán con el poder de la gente cuando vengan a reclamar la justicia. Cuando llegue ese día, acuérdate que tu suicio fue la guerra.

¡EL PODER DE LA GENTE ES MAS FUERTE QUE LAS ARMAS!

Luis A. Pérez
Ministerio de Finanza
PARTIDO DE LOS YOUNG LORDS
Sector del Bronx

PIG NO. 2

PIG HARRINGTON OF PHILADELPHIA OINKS THAT PIGS WILL FURTHER THEIR SHOOT TO KILL CAMPAIGN

PIG HARRINGTON

On Tuesday August 4,1970, a fool pig made a statement at the National Convention of the Fraternal Order of Police. This fool was John Harrington, president of the Fraternal Order of pigs, (FOP). The statement that was made by the pig was: "The pig officers may start a shoot to kill campaign if they did not receive more public support. If more public support does not materialize for pigs and if judges don't stop being permissive, then the feeling of pigs is maybe we better (sic) resort to the old Mexican deguello, a shootout in which we take no prisoners." Rizzo was there and he made a statement saying "This will never happen in Philadelphia

as long as I'm the Pig commissioner. 99 per cent of my guys would have nothing to do with something like that. We don't need that kind of thing. We, will follow the laws of the land and they apply equally to both pigs and citizens."

Now we all know that these pigs are fools. Anytime they can oink such lies to the people, knowing that the people are aware of their murder. How can Harrington say he may start something that has existed here for many years? And how can Pig Rizzo say that his pig force could never do this when they murder Black people daily in cold blood. These pigs are fools, and fools will be dealt with. We say that these pigs

do not have any respect for Black people and it is time for the people to form self defense groups throughout the Black colony. Huey says, "The pigs must withdraw immediately from the Black community and cease their wanton murder and brutality upon Black people or face the WRATH OF THE ARMED PEOPLE."

DEATH TO THE PIGS AND FOOLS!

Delores —Community Worker
Black Panther Party
Community Information Center
3625 Wallace st.
BA2-0885

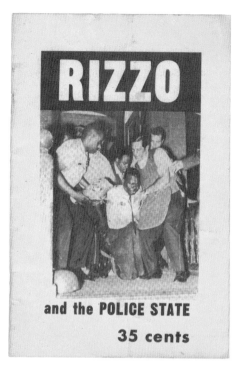

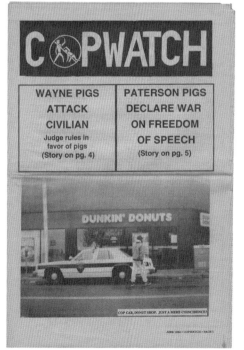

(Above) Bill Biggin, *Rizzo and the Police State* (Philadelphia, PA, Philadelphia Free Press), 1971.

Frank Rizzo was the Police Commissioner of Philadelphia from 1967-1971 and then Mayor from 1972-1980. Rizzo was a virulent racist and segregationist. As Deputy Commissioner, Rizzo led a violent raid of the Student Nonviolent Coordinating Committee (SNCC) and as Commissioner, oversaw the raid of the Black Panther Philadelphia Headquarters.

(Left) North Jersey Anarchist Federation, *CopWatch* (Haledon, NJ), newspaper, June 1992.

THE BLACK WORKER AND POLICE BRUTALITY

The Communist Party USA's affiliate group, League of Struggle for Negro Rights, later expanded to include non-Communist organizations and was known as the National Negro Congress; it put the end of police brutality and Jim Crow laws at the center of its platform. Harry Haywood, General Secretary for the League, wrote after his tours of Detroit, Cleveland, Chicago, and St. Louis that "the burning civil rights issue in these cities was police terror against the Black Community."

The League came to the defense of a Black autoworker in Detroit who was falsely accused of assaulting a white woman. Police in Detroit had begun arresting any Black person found in a white neighborhood and Haywood wrote that, "the terror campaign and the frame-up of the innocent worker had a twofold purpose: on the one hand, to intensify the

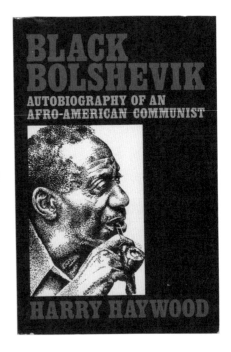

Harry Haywood, *Black Bolshevik: Autobiography of an Afro-American Communist* (Chicago, IL: Liberator Press), 1979.

oppression of Blacks and on the other, to divide and split the workers and in this way to forestall the growing tide of working class struggle against the auto lords."

Benjamin Davis, the first Black Communist Party member elected to New York City Council, wrote the pamphlet *Police Brutality, Lynching in the Northern Style* with his assistant Horace Marshall. They described police brutality in northern industrial cities as the "counterpart to lynch-terror against Negros in the semi-feudal South." Davis also wrote about how police used racial terror to break up organizing of white and Black workers. "Numerous cases of police brutality have been occasioned because Negro and white were in company together either in Harlem or other sections of the city... As the Negro people, supported by their trade union and white progressive allies, find it necessary to demonstrate, picket, and fight evictions, the policemen's billet is there to turn them back."

Horace Marshall, *Police Brutality, Lynching in the Northern Style* (New York, NY: Office of Councilman Benjamin J. Davis), 1947.

In 1951, Civil Rights Congress members Paul Robeson and William Patterson, a leader in the Communist Party USA and International Labor Defense, submitted a petition to the United Nations listing hundreds of incidents of violence against Black Americans by white supremacist groups and police. The petition, We Charge Genocide, was signed by nearly 100 activists and organizers and was meant to present an official argument that the United States government, through state-sanction violence as well as inaction in the face of discrimination, had committed genocide on Black Americans. The Civil Rights Congress was labeled a Communist organization by the House Committee of Un-American Activities (HUAC) and infiltrated by the FBI. After years of interference by US intelligence, the group disbanded in 1956. In 2014, Mariame Kaba, Todd St. Hill and other organizers in Chicago created a new We Charge Genocide petition and staged an intervention at the United Nations in Geneva with a group of eight young activists who had experienced police violence first hand. The delegation submitted a report, *Police Violence Against Chicago's Youth of Color*, to the United Nations Committee Against Torture and asked the United Nations to investigate the Chicago Police Department for its record on violence against Black people.

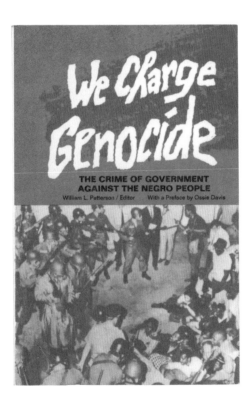

William L. Patterson, ed., *We Charge Genocide: The Crime of Government Against the Negro People* (New York: International Publishers, 1951).

20 Ways to Resist Police Violence in Chicago
Go to wechargegenocide.org/resources links and more info!

1. **Know your rights.** Read about your rights when dealing with police officers with the **National Lawyers Guild** and get trained by the **First Defense Legal Aid**
2. **Watch the cops.** Monitor the police and film encounters. It is within your rights.
3. **See something? Say Something.** If you experience or witness the cops harassing people- report it on the **Police Encounter Line**
4. **Stop calling the cops.** Check out **Chain Reaction** for ideas on alternatives to policing
5. **Defend yourself.** Call **1-800-Law-Rep-4** when someone is arrested for FREE legal defense, 24/7
6. **Help heal.** Attend a **Street Medic Training** to support political actions and your community
7. **De-militarize the CPD.** Contact your Alderman about the **Questions We Want Answered** regarding the CPD's use of military-grade weapons
8. **Decriminalize Black.** Sign the **BYP100** petition to end racially unjust marijuana arrests
9. **Stop ICE.** Endorse the **#Not1More Blue Ribbon Commission** to support immigration justice
10. **No Mandatory Minimums.** Say no to mandatory minimums, zero tolerance, and any mandatory-punishment-type laws. Sign up for action alerts with **Community Renewal Society**
11. **Justice for Roshad.** Support Dawn McIntosh, the mother of Roshad, and demand the CPD release the name of the officer who killed her son. Follow **#JusticeForRoshad**
12. **Bail people out.** Bond Davontae and LaKendra **Out of Jail** to help establish a permanent bail fund and support the community of DeSean Pittman

13. **Demand better.** Sign the **Chicago Alliance Against Racism and Political Repression** petition for an elected Civilian Police Accountability Council
14. **Reparations now.** Sign the **Chicago Torture Justice Memorials Project** ordinance petition demanding reparations for survivors of Jon Burge/CPD torture
15. **Connect inside.** Become a pen-pal to prisoners in Illinois through **Anarchist Black Cross, Black & Pink: Chicago**, or **Write to Win**
16. **Pay Attention.** Attend your neighborhood **CAPS Beat** and **Chicago Police Public Board Meetings** and disrupt harmful policies
17. **Learn.** Check out **The PIC is...** for ideas and curriculum or request a workshop from **The PIC Teaching Collective**
18. **Study.** Go to **Prison Culture** for reading lists and blog posts
19. **Build alternatives.** Learn principles and practices of participatory community justice from organizations listed on **Transform Chicago**
20. **Grow the movement.** Join, support, or donate to these and the many other incredible groups fighting for justice in our communities such as Arab American Action Network (AAAN), Chicago Alliance to Free Marissa Alexander, Chicago Childcare Collective (ChiChiCo), Chicago Revolutionary Poets Brigade, Communities United Against Foreclosures and Evictions (CUAFE), Fearless Leading by the Youth (FLY), First Defense Legal Aid, Immigrant Youth Justice League (IYJL), International Socialist Organization (ISO), the Mental Health Movement, #Not1More (NDLON), Organized Communities Against Deportations (OCAD), Project Nia, Southsiders Organized for Unity and Liberation (SOUL), Voices of Youth in Chicago Education (VOYCE) and many more!

Want to join We Charge Genocide?
New members are welcome at our monthly meetings.

Please email info@wechargegenocide.org for more information.

Concerned about police brutality in Chicago?
So are we. We are Chicago residents concerned that the epidemic of police violence continues uninterrupted in our city. Join us in monitoring & documenting police violence against Chicago's young people.

WE CHARGE GENOCIDE

REPORT POLICE MISCONDUCT ANONYMOUSLY @ https://reportencounter.wechargegenocide.org/
If you have had encounters with CPD or have witnessed CPD targeting, harassing, or abusing young people, please report the incident at the URL above.

IF YOU SEE SOMETHING, SAY #CHICOPWATCH
Join We Charge Genocide every Monday at 8pm CST for a Twitter Power Hour convo using the #chicopwatch hashtag, and use the hashtag on social media to report police harassment. For formal cop watch training, email info@wechargegenocide.org.

QUESTIONS FOR CPD & BUDGET HEARINGS
We Charge Genocide is asking the public to make sure their alderpeople ask some important questions to the Chicago Police Department when they present at the City Budget Hearings on Oct 30th. Please call and ask your alderpeople to get answers to the questions listed here: http://cpdquestions.tumblr.com/questions

WCG GENEVA DELEGATION TO THE UN
We Charge Genocide is sending a delegation of youth of color from Chicago to Geneva, Switzerland to present a report on police violence before the UN Committee Against Torture. Find out more at tinyurl.com/wcgdelegation, view the shadow report online at report.wechargegenocide.org, or donate at youcaring.com/wechargegenocide.

OCT 23RD COP WATCH & 1ST RESPONDERS TRAINING
WCG and radical medical organizers will be offering a training on legally observing & monitoring the police and how anyone can help a gunshot wound victim.
Thu, Oct 23rd, 6:30-9:30pm
Chicago Freedom School, 719 S. State St, #3N
Facebook Event: tinyurl.com/wcgoct23training

JOIN US FOR A GENERAL MEETING
Email us at info@wechargegenocide.org for location and more info.

#chicopwatch | @ChiCopWatch | wechargegenocide.org

We Charge Genocide, *20 Ways to Resist Police Violence in Chicago* (Chicago, IL), flier, 2014.

NEWSPAPER

LOS ANGELES FREE PRESS

"THE DEPUTY" REVIEWED

WILCOCK IN GREECE (AGAIN)

LIPTON: A MORALITY PLAY

136 PLACES TO GO THIS WEEK - PAGE 12

10¢

Vol. 2, #34 (Issue #57)   COPYRIGHT 1965 THE LOS ANGELES FREE PRESS   Friday, August 20, 1965   10¢ (15¢ OUTSIDE OF LOS ANGELES)

The Negroes Have Voted!

"It is always a great crime to deprive a people of its liberty on the pretext that it is using it wrongly."
DE TOQUEVILLE

L.A. TIMES, YORTY & PARKER DO NOT UNDERSTAND EVENTS

Art Kunkin

The demonstrations in the streets have completely ended the myth that the Negroes of Los Angeles are the happiest in the whole country.

It has been an election without ballot boxes and the Negroes have cast their votes. Whether or not the white majority likes this vote, it is time for the analysis which follows every election. It is time to listen to the Negro.

Attempts to simply establish "law and order," to simply establish the pre-demonstration status quo, are doomed to failure. Anyone who thinks in these terms is fundamentally anti-Negro and will be understood as such by the vast majority of Negroes.

"Law and Order"

The great tragedy is that the government officials and the major news media have not understood what has happened. They have simply seen the breakdown of "law and order" and have been showing by their statements and actions during and after the events that they did not hear the message that the Negroes were broadcasting for all with ears to hear.

Indeed the stage is now being set by the so-called responsible leaders of our community for reprisals against the Negro community, not for any positive confrontation of the problems which led thousands in Los Angeles, the "Safe City," to face death at the hands of police and soldiers because they had given up hope that ordinary democratic methods would really do anything for them and their children.

The climate locally is such that anyone who criticizes Chief Parker or the city administration for their role in the disturbances is called a Communist or a supporter of criminal elements. It is actually very dangerous in Los Angeles today to enter reasonable objections to the sensationalistic reporting and ridiculous charges of conspiracies.

Danger

Yet the voices of reason, of compassion, of immediate positive action must be heard, and it must be heard from the white community, or else the next Negro protest will be still more severe. Not only the Negro ghetto but every neighborhood in the city will become an armed camp. Not only white businesses in the ghetto will go up in flames but the very mountains and oil fields ringing Los Angeles.

And who will really be to blame then—the Negroes who act and explode out of sheer frustration, or the white community which has the power to act decisively but which did not listen before the explosion, and is not listening now?

The Los Angeles Times editorial of Tuesday, August 17, the very day the curfew ended, is a classic example of how not to listen and how to best provoke future disturbances. The Times states as one of certain "haste truths" that "What happened here was not the doing of the Negro majority in Los Angeles. Far from it. Innocent Negroes were among the saddest victims of the burning and looting." Another so-called "truth" is that "even by inference, none should condemn the criminal terrorism, or dismiss it as the inevitable result of economic and sociological pressures." The Times makes its proposals—a Governor's Commission to inquire into the causes and circumstances of the riot, and, above all, why the National Guard did not come to the scene sooner. "The Commission should be cautious of irresponsible criticism of the Los Angeles Police Department and its chief, William H. Parker.

Nonetheless, the Commission should concern itself with the possible (sic!) need of better communications between law enforcement and the Negro community . . ." Furthermore, the Times calls for "an increase in the size of the Police Department." The third Times proposal is that aid be given for the rebuilding of destroyed businesses in South Los Angeles and guarantees given them against future disorders.

No Action Proposed

The astonishing thing is that in two editorials nothing concrete and specific is said about doing anything immediately about the conditions that led to the riots.

Nothing is said about education, jobs, or housing except in terms of advice to "proceed in ordinary fashion to secure still offer advantages so long denied them." How long are people to wait, Times Editor Nick Williams and Times Publisher Chandler? It has been a super-disaster situation in the Negro ghetto for years. The people are fed up with unemployment, with subsistence on government handouts and Bureau of Public Assistance checks. The War On Poverty has done little and most of the local publicity relating to it has emphasized the haggling among politicians.

As Police Chief Parker has pointed out with some perception, "You can not keep telling them that they are being abused and mistreated without expecting them to react." But, Chief Parker, do you really think that "they" need to be told about mistreatment? Don't you recognize that "they" are being mistreated? What would you have Washington do, Chief, not even promise to (Continued on Page 3)

CORE LEADER OBSERVES GHETTO FIGHTING

Bob Freeman

On Wednesday night about 11 p.m. I arrived in Watts, a Negro ghetto in the heart of Los Angeles. Amid a hail of bottles, rocks, and stones, as an angry mob of residents, seething with resentment, was surging forth toward a group of policemen, I could hear shouting: "We will kill you, you beat and kicked that woman." "You've beat and we've been running. Who's beating who and who's running now?"

I would estimate the number taking part in this action at that time at about 1500 persons.

As I drove south on Avalon Boulevard south of Imperial Highway, I saw four police officers crouched over one man as two other officers sat on him, the officers four were beating him about the

head, arms and shoulders with billy clubs. To my left approached a crowd, shouting "Don't kill that man!"

The crowd began to attack the officers as the officers responded with "Shut up, dirty niggers" and "You better get out of here and go home, niggers." Just then the crowd came closer and began to attack the officers. The officers first attempted to fight back but then ran away.

As I drove south another block I saw four officers approach one Negro who was walking along the sidewalk empty handed. One officer said, "Come here, nigger." As the man turned, the officers jumped him and began to beat him.

He fell on the ground, but instantaneously the crowd was there running the officers off.

I felt then it was wise to park my car and inquire of some of the people on the street what had happened to start this. I approached two men who had just discharged their last stones and bottles and asked my question.

They replied that the cops had stopped some man about a traffic violation. Two women had approached the scene and during the ensuing events the officers had knocked one of the women to the ground and hit and kicked her. They said this had enraged the crowd which had been looking on. While enroute to Watts I had

(Continued on page 2)

RIOT!

So far we've looked at communities consciously organizing to protest police violence and racial injustice, but some major turning points in the national conversation about policing happened not after organized protests but in response to spontaneous, large-scale riots.

The police beating of 21-year-old Marquette Frye and arrest of his mother Rena Price ignited the Watts Rebellion in 1965, which lasted for six days. The National Guard arrived on the third day to quell the uprising and 34 people were killed, almost all by law enforcement. Congress of Racial Equality (CORE) member Bob Freeman gave a first-hand account of the uprising in the *LA Free Press* and editor Art Kunkin wrote, "the great tragedy is that the government officials and the major news media have not understood what has happened. They have simply seen the breakdown of 'law and order'.... Indeed

the stage is now being set by the so-called responsible leaders of our community for reprisals against the Negro community, not for any positive confrontation of the problems which led thousands in Los Angeles, the 'Safe City,' to face death at the hands of police."

In 1967, the beating of John William Smith sparked riots in Newark, just one of 159 riots that took place that summer in response to police brutality. Eventually known as the Long Hot Summer, riots in 1967 resulted in 85 deaths and over 11,000 arrests nationwide. This prompted President Johnson's administration to create the Commission on Civil Disorders, known more commonly as the Kerner Commission, which attributed unrest to years of housing discrimination, exclusion from the job market, and white racism. The Commission concluded, "segregation and

LOS ANGELES

press, there really was significant racism in the widespread looting of Korean owned businesses. Korean shops were clearly singled out for looting.

There are many factors that contribute to the animosity between the Black and Korean communities. African-Americans living in LA constitute a minority amongst minorities. The Hispanic and Asian communities are both growing rapidly, and many Blacks feel like they're being pushed out. The Asian, Hispanic and Black communities are pitted against each other in a battle to survive. The beating of Rodney King was just one incident that primed the Black community of Los Angeles for revolt. Perhaps equally important was the shooting in the back of 14 year old Latasha Harlins by a Korean shop-owner who was let off with probation and community service.

This antagonism was exploited by the police, who facilitated the attacks on Korean shops by arresting armed Korean shop-owners while protecting white owned businesses.

The hyped incidents of attacks on whites or Asians, while inexcusable, need to be put into perspective: compare four incidents in over a week with the average number of racists assaults by the LAPD in one day! And, in each case, not only did the majority of people condemn the attacks as misdirected and wrong, but individuals — without guns, nightsticks or stinking badges — intervened, at their own personal risk, and directly stopped them. (And not like Officer Briseno, the "turncoat" cop, claimed he helped Rodney King by stomping on his back to get him to stay still.)

But these examples are evidence of misdirection — or maybe stupidity or even malice — but certainly not of the "mindlessness" or "randomness" of the violence. On the other hand, even in the reports from the usual unreliable sources, it was obvious that much of the rage was strikingly well directed: police cars, police stations and the police themselves were prime targets. So were government offices, banks, large chain stores...and gunshops.

CAUSES OF THE REBELLION

The rebellion was righteous despite some ugliness.

While people of many different backgrounds participated in the action, poorer African Americans led the way because they have the least to lose.

Many African Americans face unemployment, or have low paying, go-nowhere jobs. Many are unable to obtain the basic necessities of life: decent housing, health care, food. Black people face discrimination in getting education and jobs.

People of color have an extremely high probability of being put in prison. Of Black men between the ages 20 and 29, 1 in 4 will go to prison or be placed on probation. 60% of the wimmin in prison are wimmin of color. Poverty and the absence of other opportunities to escape it compel many Black youth to turn to gangs, drugs, and anti-social crime. An estimated 150,000 youth belong to the roughly 1,000 LA gangs. Half of all Black and Hispanic youth of South Central LA belong to gangs. In central LA, half of the Black families fall below the poverty line, and youth unemployment hovers at 50%.

In LA there is a widespread sense that community leaders and a Black political establishment betrayed the community. There were tensions building before the verdict, ie, the standoff between Police Chief Darryl Gates and Mayor Tom Bradley. After the beating of King, the police commission suspended Gates, but the city council reinstated him, appeasing pro-police white voters.

In July of 1991, Gates promised to resign by April of '92, but was still in office when the trial verdict was released (actually, he wasn't in his office, he was at a fundraiser). In short, the wimpiness of the mayor and white liberals showed clearly when compared to the political power of Gates. At a meeting at the First A.M.E. Church during the first hours of rioting, the mayor, clergy, and community leaders were booed and ignored by much of the audience. A young black womyn charged the podium, and took control of the mike. "We can't rely on these people up here to act...I believe they have our best interests at heart, but we cannot rely on them...You know what we need to do."

DON'T BELIEVE THE HYPE

The poor of LA had little to lose. Is it any surprise people reacted the way that they did? The plight of the poor is usually ignored. For the past 12 years politicians have succeeded in demonizing Blacks. From the Willie Horton ad designed to transform racist fear into votes for Bush, to the racial code words of "welfare," "crime," and "affirmative action," an atmosphere of vicious racism has been consciously cultivated by conservatives and liberals alike.

The result of this is that there is no longer a War on Poverty, but an outright War on the Poor in the disguises of the war on drugs, crime prevention, reforming welfare, etc. Racism, oppression, and the politics that divide people are what capitalism thrives on, and what maintains this white supremacist system. The rebellion in LA was a bold rejection of "business as usual." It was to be expected, not condemned.

The old racist lies of recent political campaigns have been transformed into new racist lies about the rebellion. Politicians and the capitalist media would have us believe that people were consciously burning down their own homes in some irrational expression of rage. Certainly, people's homes were burnt down. Fires set to more deserving targets sometimes accidentally spread to people's homes. Some people's homes may have been set on fire deliberately. We are not in a position to know to what degree these incidents involved deserving targets. What we do know is that the portrayal of the Black community of Los Angeles as so insane as to destroy their own homes is propaganda designed to dehumanize that community and prepare us for the brutal repression that followed the rebellion.

THE EMPIRE STRIKES BACK

The Los Angeles revolt and the shock waves that spread around the world struck fear in the hearts of the US ruling elite. Almost immediately they began to strike back. The invasion of Los Angeles first by National Guard and then by Federal troops reflected that war had broken out in Los Angeles, and that the longer the revolt lasted the further it might spread. A curfew was established and basic civil liberties were suspended. The California courts extended the period of time people could be held under arrest without charge from 24 hours to a full week. Over 14,000 people were arrested in Los Angeles. Over 1,000 people were deported as "illegal aliens." Over 2,000 people were arrested in sweeps in the San Francisco Bay area, at least half of whom were clearly engaged only in peaceful protest. The National Guard was mobilized in Las Vegas as well.

The military and police response to the revolt went right along with the effective use of television for social control. At first, the television news eagerly broadcast helicopter shots of the early hours of the revolt. But as it became clear that the Los Angeles uprising was no ordinary riot, that it was sweeping the second largest city in the US, and becoming the largest single expression of domestic unrest since the Civil War, the televisicn coverage shifted to damage-control mode. The spread of the unrest to every corner of the country could not be denied, so it was reduced to short clips without meaningful information about the scale of the revolt, mixed with lengthier accounts of "socially acceptable" expressions of protest. Every hour we were assured that calm was returning, that law and order were being restored.

Every effort was made to chill out the militancy of the moment. When Berkeley High School students marched on a police station, the police issued a statement in support of the demonstration. In Minneapolis, a coelition lead largely by the Socialist Workers Party negotiated with the police to prevent any violence, to keep the massive police mobilization out of view (but not so far away that they could not attack), but the Chief of Police and prominent pro-police politicians were allowed to join the march unmolested.

Then Hollywood got in on the act. Actors attracted massive media attention for performing the mundane tasks of cleaning up. The revolt was being recuperated by the spectacle, transformed from the act of thousands of people reclaiming control over their lives to a topic for commentary by Tom Petty, Arsenio Hall, and the predictable array of politicians and journalists.

THE WAR AT HOME

But the Los Angeles revolt was not a movie. It was a real event in the lives of real people. It was the collective expression of a community that had been oppressed and brutalized for too long, and had decided to fight back. The jurors in Simi Valley explained that they based their verdict acquitting the four cops charged with beating Rodney King on more than the 81 seconds of videotape that the whole world had seen. They said they based it on what happened before the video-taped beating. They meant 15 minutes before — not 400 years before.

There was a tremendous amount of anger expressed across the country, revealing the depth of the crisis in our society. What happened in LA over a week was an intensified version of what's been going on all along. When people are enslaved, caged, beaten and denied the basics of life, they react in many ways. Some seek revenge, some to fulfill their needs, some kill. 10,000 business destroyed, 58 dead, nearly 10,000 arrested, a billion dollars worth of damage.

An increasingly fascist USA has intensified its war on Blacks, taking back the crumbs, changing the rules of government aid to punish. There's been a long history of injustice that led up to what happened in Los Angeles. From the time of slavery to the present, Africans living in America have struggled for their freedom. The events in Los Angeles were the continuation of this struggle. The verdict in the trial of officers Wind, Koon, Briseno and Powell confirmed and reiterated the truth — that there is still no justice for African Americans. The reaction of LA's Black community was a clear sign that the fight will not end until there is justice.

Black people have been fighting back against a system so deeply racist that it can only be understood as a form of domestic colonialism. Brought here as slaves, Blacks have remained, as a community, economically subordinate to a white economic elite, like a colony under foreign occupation. Forced into ghettos or dispersed in housing projects, the Black community is subjected to police and judicial practices that closely resemble colonial military occupation. Police forces in every major city are trained in counter-insurgency techniques perfected by the British and US militaries in their wars against Third World national liberation movements. Black men make up 46% of the US prison population. The drug trade and accompanying violence have been used to systematically tear apart whatever kind of cohesive community Black people have been able to create. These communities have not been allowed to be self-sufficient, so some people took things into their own hands.

The dispatch of the Army, Marines, National Guard and more police could be viewed as merely the sending in of reinforcements for a war that's seen many battles. The Los Angeles revolt needs to be understood historically. It needs to be seen as part of a continuing struggle. It also needs to be seen as the serious departure from the previous terms of that struggle that it is. A good place to start to understand what happened in Los Angeles in 1992 is to remember the Watts rebellion of 1965.

WATTS UP DOC?

In the summer of 1965, the Watts area of Los Angeles rose up in revolt. The Watts revolt was the first major urban uprising of the 1960s. It signalled a new phase in the struggle for Black liberation. The Civil Rights movement that had arisen in the South was unable to speak effectively to the needs of urban Black communities elsewhere. Like the recent Los Angeles uprising, the Watts revolt was sparked by an incident involving police violence, but reflected a much deeper alienation from US society, indeed from capitalism as a system. The Watts revolt was the beginning of a revolutionary phase for the Black movement. The revolutionary Black movement that emerged in the following years took the form of both more spontaneous uprisings (Detroit and Newark in 1967, everywhere in 1968), and the creation of organizations like the Black Panther Party, the League of Revolutionary Black Workers, and others. By the early 1970s this movement had been effectively crushed by state repression where it had not been torn apart by its own internal tensions.

It is not unlikely that the coming years will see more urban uprisings or even the establishment of popular revolutionary Black organizations. There are many differences between the current situation and the situation in the 1960s, but knowing what happened then can help us respond more effectively to events

PAGE 4 • LOVE AND RAGE • JUNE 1992

"Revolt: the choice of a new generation," *Love & Rage* (New York, NY), newspaper, 1992.

The Fire This Time

this time around. By studying the events of that period we can see how the movement exploited or failed to exploit the crises that were pulling the system in different directions.

One of the big differences between the Watts rebellion and the more recent Los Angeles revolt is the political context in which the two events took place. Watts was in many ways an expression of the failure of the civil rights movement in the South to speak to the economic issues confronting the urban Black communities of the North. But, by the same token, it took place in the context of that movement. There were sections of the civil rights movement who were able to rise to the occasion and organize a more militant and revolutionary Black liberation movement. When the founders of the Oakland based Black Panther Party took the Black Panther symbol from the Mississippi-base Lowndes County Freedom Organization it was an expression of the continuity that existed with the earlier Southern phase of the civil rights movement.

"The Crenshaw shopping district, the heart of L.A.'s Black middle class and the only significant commercial district in South Central had burned to the ground."

Village Voice

In 1965 there was not much of a Black middle class. One of the consequences

of the urban revolts of the 1960s was the creation of a larger Black middle class to serve as a buffer for what remained a white supremacist system. During the recent rebellion, this new Black middle class was also targeted by the people.

In 1992 there does not exist a movement in the Black community that compares to the civil rights movement of the 1960s. This does not mean that people will not create such a movement. It does mean that a new movement is likely to reflect more deeply a rejection of the liberal integrationist politics of the traditional civil rights movement. The question of Black self-determination is likely to take a more prominent place beside more traditional demands for civil rights in any resurgent Black movement. The civil rights movement has failed the Black community in its promise to bring Blacks into the mainstream of a white supremacist society. The establishment of forces of Black autonomous power, from organizations of struggle to educational institutions, will be a priority in the coming period.

BLACK POWER AND THE CLASS WAR

The revolt that rocked Los Angeles had both racial and class characteristics. Chicanos, whites, and others partici-

pated in what was none the less mainly a Black uprising. While it is important to see how the spirit of revolt that surged forward in the Black community can be spread to the rest of the working class and to other oppressed peoples, it is also important to acknowledge what the Los Angeles revolt demonstrates so clearly: the centrality of the fight for Black liberation to any revolutionary movement in the US. Try to imagine a white working class community rising up tomorrow like South Central Los Angeles and the situation becomes clear.

Many white Americans, when faced with the struggles of African Americans, are unable or unwilling to deal with their own racism. White working class communities, even the poorest ones, lack the history of revolt, the culture of resistance, the sense of common antagonism with the police that characterizes most Black communities. While most working class whites will never escape their class standing, the possibility is a thousand times greater than for most Black people. The poorest white person can imagine themselves owning a small store under the existing system, and therefore feels they have something to lose when they see revolts like those that rocked Los Angeles. This sentiment is considerably less widespread in the Black community. The popularity of anti-police rap songs among black youth does not have a parallel among white youth.

Millions of people, who live lives very different from the people of South Central Los Angeles, felt a thrill at the sight of the revolt. That instinct towards solidarity is what needs to be transformed into a broad revolutionary movement. All sorts of people across the US (and around the world) responded to the revolt. This sense of solidarity reflects the potential among many sectors of society for revolt. It also indicates the importance of the Black community, since no other community has demonstrated the power to inspire such widespread revolt. We want to build a revolutionary movement that includes all sectors of the working class and all other deeply oppressed under this system. Making supporting the Black liberation movement a priority is a strategic decision based on the understanding that the Black liberation movement has a unique potential to inspire revolutionary action across this society.

The revolt in Los Angeles will very likely push forward the development of revolutionary forces within the Black community. These forces may remain relatively small, or they may grow dramatically. Either way, they will need support. They will become the immediate targets of state repression. If we are serious about building a broad and

multi-racial revolutionary movement, now is the time to provide concrete support for Black revolutionaries. At the same time we need to build on the sense of solidarity with the revolt that was expressed in many other communities. There is a fight going on right now for the conscience of white America. For a moment, millions of white people were clearly in the Rodney King verdict the brutal injustice that is the daily experience of Black people in the US. ABC News reported that 39% of white Americans believe that the government "only responds to blacks when they resort to violence." Many saw in the revolt an expression of righteous anger, and many poured into the streets to express their outrage as well.

This momentary expression of solidarity scares the hell out of the powers-that-be who are working furiously to reverse it. The reversal will take two forms: liberal cooptation with promises of new social programs, and outright racist reaction. We need to fight back against both. We need to uphold the revolt, not just as an expression of righteous outrage, but as an opening round in what we hope will be a rising tide of popular uprisings. The revolt should not be a wake-up call for the ruling class, so that they can throw the poor a few more crumbs. It should be a wake-up call for the oppressed, showing the possibility of a revolutionary solution to our problems. We also need to take up the fight against racism within white working class communities. Black people are not the only people looking for a radical way out of the present situation. A growing fascist movement in white communities is also speaking to many people's deep fears. We need to be in those communities to challenge this movement, to build solidarity with the Black liberation movement, and to cultivate a spirit of revolt that sees in the uprisings in the Black community the beginnings of an even broader struggle for a world worth living in.

SPONTANEOUS REVOLT AND PREPARATIONS FOR REVOLUTION

But the need for such preparations should not be confused with the acceptance of any bunch of self-appointed leaders claiming to know what's best for the people.

Perhaps most positive of all was the real festivity evident — created cooperatively among a large, diverse, multiracial populace taking control for themselves for once. It was a brief moment that was enormously far from being able to last, let alone grow, but we still find it inspiring.

It is also challenging and frightening, for it forces us to ask: how can the tremendous changes necessary to actually start achieving anarchy ever come about, and what, if anything, can anarchists do to speed them? The people of South Central Los Angeles were able to perform amazing feats with very little formal organization. Contrary to the lies about turning on their own community, people invaded Hollywood and Beverly Hills, striking at the rich who have made their lives miserable, in a way that has not been seen in many previous urban uprisings. But, on the most elemental level, the moment passed because the cops — with the aid of over 10,000 state police, Army, Marines, and National Guards — were able to regain and hold control of the streets. Although scattered driveby shootings of cops and guards, among other forms of resistance, continued for several weeks in Los Angeles and a few other places like Las Vegas, all the large scale uprisings were put down within a few days. The people did not have the capacity to effectively resist the military occupation of their communities, either by direct confrontation, guerilla activity, or by spreading the rebellion into the ranks of the Army and National Guard. The media blackout succeeded in limiting the spread of revolt. A strong revolutionary media could have broken the blackout. Recent events have shown that mass

urban uprisings are one way to challenge the state's power. Defeating it will take a more sustained, determined, organized struggle.

Unless there are already at least seeds of truly collective, non-hierarchal organization at a directly democratic level to consciously oppose authoritarian methods, these will come out on top, particularly in a military situation.

Then the fact must be faced that looting has only very short-term viability as a supply solution. Very soon inventories are depleted and then must be restocked, stuff grown, moved around, etc. — and if domination is to be ended, this must all be organized directly, democratically and collectively by all those involved in the doing. But surely, it can't be the same things made the same way, the same stuff grown where and how it was, all moved to and from the same places by the same methods. We — all participating individuals, around the world — will have to re-examine and re-do everything.

Is the leap from here to there possible, let alone probable? We don't know. Those who'd like to see it happen can and should do something to make it more possible/probable. We can't — and shouldn't try to — create non-hierarchal collectives spanning the cities from ghetto to barrio. We can and should organize ourselves, directly, non-hierarchically, on the level we can, beginning with affinity groups and political collectives. We can't — and shouldn't try to — build people's militias; we can — and should — take seriously (though not humorlessly) our encounters with the cops, learning what we can, going as far as we can, and preparing for tomorrow. We can't decide how production and distribution should be reorganized, but we can and should study and investigate various alternatives, not simply as theories (although that has its merit), but in really creating alternative models for housing, childcare, health, food supply, entertainment, communication, etc, etc. (and learning from those, such as Food Not Bombs, Wimmin's self-health collectives, etc., which already exist).

Undoubtedly this analysis is insufficient and incomplete. We do not doubt that we suffer from misinformation and misperceptions of what has been occurring. Nonetheless, it's important for anarchists to understand and learn from what has happened; we hope others will correct, add to, and contradict these ideas. ✦

This article was spliced together from a couple of different sources. Gene, Dema, and Chris of the Production Group worked on an article together, and did the final putting together. Substantial portions of an article written by Bruce Kais were included, and lots of information came from the many and excellent reports we got from around North America and around the world. (Look for all of those in the discussion bulletin.)

poverty have created in the racial ghetto a destructive environment totally unknown to most white Americans. What white Americans have never fully understood but what the Negro can never forget—is that white society is deeply implicated in the ghetto. White institutions created it, white institutions maintain it, and white society condones it." The Commission recommended increased spending for social programs in major cities, which Johnson resisted and Richard Nixon later used as a cudgel against Democrats during his "law-and-order" presidential campaign.

In May 1991, the Mount Pleasant neighborhood in Washington, DC exploded into a riot after the police shot a Salvadoran man, Daniel Enrique Gomez, in the chest at the tail end of Cinco de Mayo celebrations. The neighborhood was home to a large Central American population and in response to the shooting, hundreds of Salvadoran, Nicaraguan, and Honduran youth fought pitched battles with the police and smashed and looted storefronts. Riots went on for multiple nights—with Black and white youth joining in—and exposed large-scale hatred for, and distrust of, the police within DC's communities of color, particularly amongst young people.

Just prior to these events, Los Angeles police had been caught on tape brutally beating Rodney King. When the officers involved were acquitted on April 29th, 1992, huge swaths of the Black community in LA rioted for six days and nights, leading to the deaths

March and Mass
For Dignity and Justice
Wednesday July 15 1992

OUR COMMUNITY DEMANDS:

Dismissal, Arrest and Trial of the police officers involved in the deaths of Jose " Kiko " Garcia and Dagoberto Pichardo.

MORE JOBS, EDUCATION, HOUSING AND HEALTH SERVICES.

March: 162 St & Saint Nicholas . 6 PM
Mass: 172 St & Audubon Avenue. 7 PM

Wear black as a sign of mourning.

Sponsored by :
COMMITTEE AGAINST POLICE BRUTALITY.
For information call: (212) 543-1047 / 231-0506.

MARCHA Y MISA
POR LA DIGNIDAD Y JUSTICIA
Miércoles 15 de julio de 1992

NUESTRA COMUNIDAD DEMANDA:

EL DESPIDO, ARRESTO Y ENJUICIAMIENTO DE LOS POLICIAS IMPLICADOS EN LOS ASESINATOS DE JOSE "KIKO" GARCIA Y DAGOBERTO PICHARDO.

MAS SERVICIOS DE SALUD, EDUCACION, VIVIENDA Y TRABAJOS.

Marcha: Calle 162 y Saint Nicholas . 6 PM
Misa : Calle 172 y Avenida Audubon . 7 PM

Vístase de negro como señal de luto.

Auspicia:
COMITE CONTRA LA BRUTALIDAD POLICIAL.
Para más información llamar al (212) 543-1047 / 231-0506.

Committee Against Police Brutality, *March and Mass for Dignity and Justice / Marcha y Misa Por la Dignidad y Justicia* (New York, NY), flier, 1992.

The deaths of Jose 'Kiko' Garcia and Dagoberto Pichardo at the hands of the police sparked riots in Washington Heights in July 1992.

State of Emergency

Black Youth! Stand and Fight!

**From South Africa to LA to Washington Heights,
The Murders continue.....**

Black Unity Rally to Stop the Killings

July 11, 1992 at 3:00 PM

Grand Army Plaza Flatbush Ave. & Eastern Parkway
#2,3,4,5, to Grand Army Plaza - D to 7th ave

Sponsored by: The Black Consciousness Movement, Black Consciousness Movement of
Azania, The Malcolm X Grassroots Movement, Fuerza Latina and Black Nia Force
For further information call: (718) 712-5447

The Black Consciousness Movement, Black Consciousness Movement of Azania, The Malcolm X Grassroots
Movement, Fuerza Latina and Black Nia Force, *Black Unity Rally to Stop the Killings* (New York, NY), flier, 1992.

of 63 people, over 2,000 injured, and over $1 billion in property damage. The LA uprising was the largest of its kind since the Watts Rebellion. These events, and the media circulation of the bystander video of King's beating, awoke the rest of the US not only to widespread police abuse within communities of color, but to the level of frustration, anger, and hatred held against the police within poor and working-class communities. Although the person who shot the footage of the King beating was not a formal member of CopWatch, the effect of the video showed how powerful the tactic could be in organizing a response to police violence.

#BlackLivesMatter (#BLM) became a hashtag after the 2013 acquittal of George Zimmerman for the killing of teenager Trayvon Martin and gained wider recognition after the police killings of Michael Brown in Ferguson, MO, and Eric Garner in New York City. It quickly moved from an online protest to a network of autonomous activist groups on the ground, and for the first time in decades the criminalization of Black people became part of the national conversation. After massive protests in 2014, cities responded with familiar reformist attempts: New York's Civilian Complaint Review Board requested more robust roles in police oversight, including having the authority to fire policemen and change department policies. President Barack Obama initiated the President's Task Force on 21st Century Policing, with representation from multiple groups active in the Movement for Black Lives. Like the 1968 Kerner Commission before it, their report examined community relationships to police and provided recommendations, from diversifying the police force to classifying use-of-force

Love & Rage, Vol 3 No 5 (New York, NY), newspaper, 1992, cover.

policies. Ultimately, it was up to individual municipalities to adopt the suggestions put forth by the Task Force and, while a few major cities did, death rates at the hands of police have remained stubbornly consistent, even as overall crime rates have largely dropped over the past two decades.

Mazatl & Dignidad Rebelde, *I Am Trayvon Martin and My Life Matters* (Oakland, CA) screenprint poster, 2013.

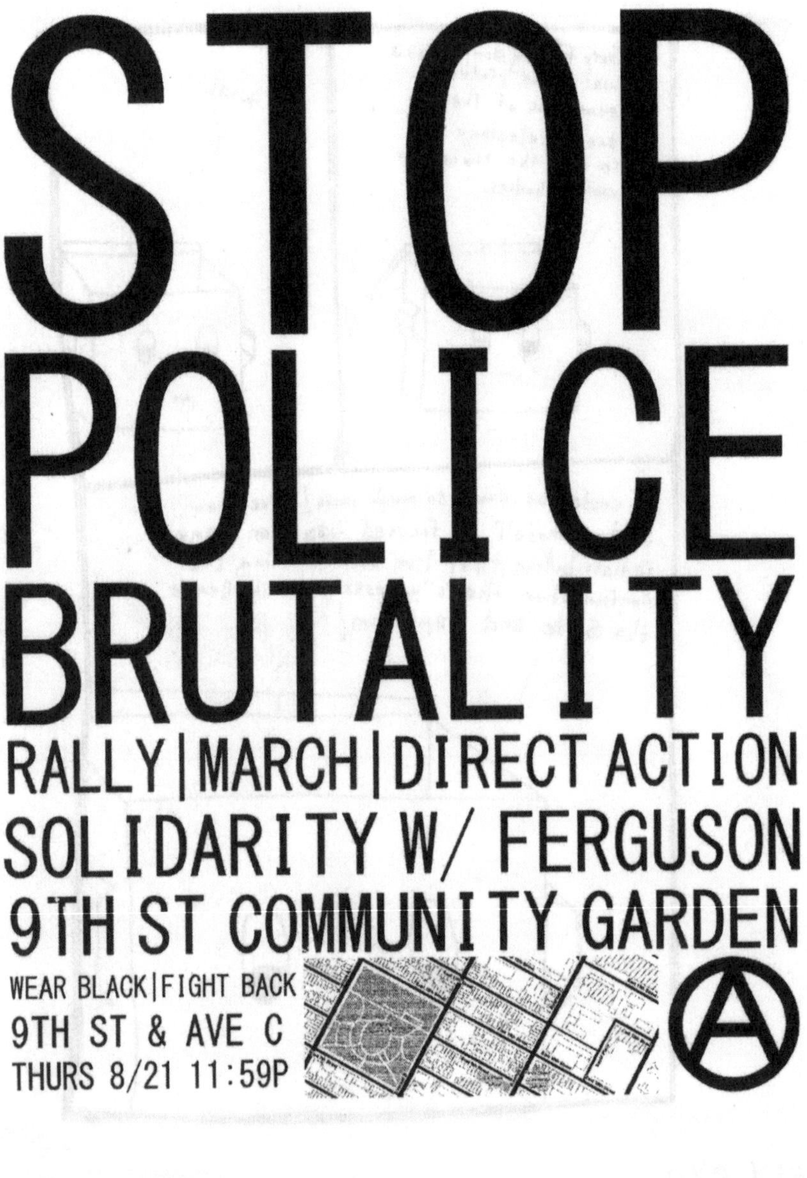

STOP POLICE BRUTALITY

RALLY|MARCH|DIRECT ACTION
SOLIDARITY W/ FERGUSON
9TH ST COMMUNITY GARDEN

WEAR BLACK|FIGHT BACK
9TH ST & AVE C
THURS 8/21 11:59P

Stop Police Brutality Rally/Stand with Ferguson (New York, NY), flier, 2014.

(Left) Ferguson October, *Ferguson Needs You*, flier, 2014.

(Below) Black Lives Matter, *Black Lives Matter*, poster, 2014.

BLACK LIVES MATTER

WWW.BLACKLIVESMATTER.COM

Have you ever been attacked, harassed, beaten, insulted ... by the cops?

Come to a SPEAK OUT

In the spirit of Stonewall, help build resistance against police abuse.

Saturday, Sept. 29
2:00–7:00

*Wheelchair Accessible
*ASL Interpretation
*Childcare

The Lesbian and Gay Community Services Center
208 W. 13th St. (7th/8th) in Manhattan

807-7269 or
691-7950 x6102

This speak-out is being called by the Anti-Police Abuse Coalition (APAC) whose members include individuals and representatives of Black and White Men Together/NY Political Action Committee; Dykes Against Racism Everywhere (DARE); Freedom Socialist Party; John Brown Anti-Klan Committee; Libertarians for Gay and Lesbian Concerns; Lambda Legal Defense and Education Fund; National Coalition of Black Gays; Radical Women; All Peoples Congress Lesbian and Gay Focus; Venceremos Brigade/NY Regional.

EVERYONE IS WELCOME

DARE
Dykes Against Racism Everywhere

CAN YOU PICTURE
YOURSELF IN THIS
SCENE?

| P.O. Box 914 | Stuyvesant Station | New York City, NY 10009 | (212) 691-7950 x6102 |

Dykes Against Racism Everywhere (DARE) *Have you been attacked, harassed, beaten, insulted...by the cops?* (New York, NY) poster, 1979.

QUEER RESISTANCE

Beginning in at least the 19th century, many municipalities across the country had laws prohibiting subversive gender expression. Sodomy laws existed in all states until gradual decriminalization in the 1970s and 1980s and eventual national repeal in 2003. Gay men and women, gender queer people, and sex workers were routinely harassed by police, targeted in clubs, imprisoned and abused, and were not afforded the same protection under the law when they experienced violence.

The anti-police riot at Stonewall is often cited as the beginning of the gay liberation movement, but the Cooper Do-nuts riot in 1959, the Black Cat protest in 1967 in Los Angeles, and the Compton's Cafeteria riot in San Francisco in 1966 all preceded Stonewall. Queer people were also organizing in informal ways, creating safe communities and providing shelter and resources for one another.

Street Transvestite Action Revolutionaries (STAR), founded by Sylvia Rivera and Marsha P. Johnson, was formed in 1970 just a year after Stonewall. It was known for STAR House, a place for homeless queer youth, addicts, and sex workers. Their work paved the way for many trans-led mutual aid efforts today. The STAR platform resembles the 10 Point Platform of the Black Panther Party and includes the demand for autonomy from the violent state and the end of police harassment. STAR and a number of other queer-led organizations went to the capitol of New York in 1971 to protest cross-dressing and gender vice laws.

(Left) Molly Crabapple, *Free Marissa* (New York City), button.
(Right) Molly Crabapple, *Defend Black Girls Now* (New York City), button.

Organizing by trans people of color has continued at the forefront of queer resistance to police brutality, notably through campaigns to free incarcerated Black trans people including CeCe McDonald, Ashley Diamond, Eisha Love, and Ky Peterson. Organizations like Survived & Punished and Southerners on New Ground led campaigns to free these and other trans men and women who were convicted for defending themselves against abusers and rapists and were denied trans-inclusive medical care in prison facilities. Activists pushed to repeal New York and California's "walking while trans" laws, which were "loitering" laws designed to police sex workers and disproportionately criminalized Black, Latinx, and Indigenous trans women.

Since the mid-1990s, LGBTQ Pride parades have become more mainstream, state-sanctioned, and friendly to both politicians and corporate sponsors. Organizations like the trans youth-led FIERCE! and the Transgender Gender-Variant Intersex Justice Project (TGIJP), founded by Miss Major and Alexander Lee in San Francisco, have protested the presence of police at Pride parades and have called attention to the continual criminalization of queers living in poverty, trans women of color, and sex workers. After the PULSE nightclub shooting in Orlando, Florida in 2016, Bay Area Black Lives Matter pulled out of the San Francisco Pride Parade and TGIJP joined them in protest of increased police presence and security.

TV'S AND QUEENS

MARCH ON ALBANY

Seek Statute to Legalize Crossdressing!

"Grant us courage for the facing of this hour," stung the drag queens, tv's and homosexuals attending the church services prior to the march on the State Capital in Albany, Sunday, March 14th. The march was in support of the bills currently before the legislators in behalf of liberalized laws on homosexuality. Amongst them are bill for the repeal of impersonation laws, according to the Gay Activists Alliance news release.

This is the first time in the history of the homophile movement that the gay organizations have publicly acknowledged as one of their goals the legalization of female impersonation.

Queens Liberation Front supporters, S.T.A.R. (Street Transvestites Action Revolutionaries) and their guests went to Albany on one of the four buses chartered by the NY GAA, slowly marched out of the church with the song still ringing in their ears and tears in their eyes..."Grant us courage for the facing of this hour......"

Albany is known for its small town

attitudes so the demonstrators didn't know what their reaction would be to the three thousand invaders. Would they allow the gays to demonstrate without any trouble? Would the drag queen and tv be arrested? How did they feel about the invasion? According to one of the N.Y. newspapers, "Well, they loved Lee Brewster, anyway... Lee displayed 'her' womanly charms to stupified firemen and their hardhat buddies." The Albany KNICK-EOCHER NEWS reported the demonstration and speeches in their article, "We're not afraid anymore", the signature line of the Rev. Troy Perry. Womens Lib Leader, Kate Millet, Lee G. Brewster of QLF and the Rev. Troy Perry were quoted in the article.

Amongst the QUEENS delegation was Bunny Eisenhower who explained to passersby why he dressed. His wife was with him and contributed to his defense and the two enlightened many. Bobbie, who gives drag balls and dances and his friend carried the QUEENS banner during the entire march.

The town was stunned but no trouble occured. After the demonstration the participants returned to New York feeling a spirit of unity and satisfaction. ∎

S.T.A.R. (Street Transvestite Action Revolutionaries) was out in full force for the demonstration. Standing next to Lee Brewster is Sylvia Rivera leader of the militant transvestite group.

Sylvia (S.T.A.R.) and Lee (Q.L.F.) lead the march on the capitol. Both militant transvestites spoke to the press and 3,000 spectators. The Rev. Troy Perry also spoke.

Bunny and wife after a long trip.   Even the kids were for us! ∎

VOL # I NO III

"TV's and Queens March on Albany Seek Statute to Legalize Crossdressing!" *Drag Queens: A Magazine about Transvestites*, Volume I No III, p 30, 33. (New York, NY), pamphlet, 1971.

♀♀ GAY NEWS ♂♂

LISA JIMENEZ & EVELYN RIVERA VS. TRANSIT POLICE

EVELYN RIVERA

On Dec. 28, 1986, just 8 days after the Howard Beach incident Lisa Jimenez & Evelyn Rivera encountered homophobic and racially motivated police brutality Traveling south on the No. 2, IRT train in the Bronx, five men attacked their gay male friend (Danny Velasquez) – they beer-bathed and beat him. The transit officer who first arrived at the scene, proceeded to arrest Danny while Evelyn protested and pointed out Danny's bloodied face and the fact that they had summoned police help for him. The officer replied nastily, "Shut the fuck up."

As other officers arrived, Evelyn states she overheard the first-comer tell another officer, while pointing at her, "That bitch there is mine".

Summarily, six officers went to arrest Evelyn and Lisa, who had also tried reasoning with the officers. In the end, one woman was knocked unconscious while the other needed six stitches to her forehead. Other bruises were also sustained by both women. While pinned to the ground, Evelyn noted that the officers called her "dyke", "spic", and "bitch".

While detained at the 41st precinct, only one officer was kind enough to bring them coffee, and tea, etc...regularly.

All charges against the two women have been dropped except for " verbal obstruction of justice", which carries a one year jail sentence. On JAN 19, 1988, Judge Roger Hunting will hear their case. If the charges are not dismissed, they could be sentenced. Please support Lisa & Evelyn by being there: JURY PART 7.

BRONX CRIMINAL COURT, 215 E. 161st St., BRONX, N.Y. 10451 * 9:30 A.M.

You can also write the above address and ask Hon. Judge Roger Hunting to dismiss the charge of "verbal obstruction of justice".

****

SHESCAPE & COMPLAINANTS REACH SETTLEMENT

At last, Shescape Prod., Inc. and the 9 complainants who filed with the N.Y.C. Human Rights Commission alleging racial discrimination in Shescape admissions practices during late 1985 and 1986 (by documentation as filed) have reached an accord. A Joint Statement has been issued by both parties, check with your gay/women presses (Womanews, GCN, N.Y. Native, etc./or bookstores), or call COOL for a copy.

If you'd like to make more COOL things happen or have uncool incidents to report contact:

Committee of Outraged Lesbians
204 W. 20th St., R-93, NY NY 10011
212/243-0202

Committee of Outraged Lesbians, *Gay News* (New York, NY), pamphlet, 1987.

STREET TRANSVESTITES ACTION REVOLUTIOARIES

The oppression against transvestite of either sex aries from sexist values
and this oppression is manifested by hetrosexuals and homosexual of both
sexes in form of exploitation, ridicule,harrassment,beatings, rapes,
murders.

Because of this oppression the majority of transvestites are forced into
the streets we have have framed a strong alliance with our gay sisters
and brothers of the street. Who we are a part of and represent we are;
a part of the revolutionaries armies fighting against the system.

1.We want the right to self-determination over the use of our bodies;
the right to be gay, anytime, anyplace; the right to free physiological
change and modification of sex on demand; the right to free dress and
adornment.

2.The end to all job discrimination against transvestites of both sexes and
gay street people because of attire.

3.The immediate end of all police harrassment and arrest of transvestites
and gay street people, and the release of transvestites and gay street
people from all prisons and all other political prisoners.

4.The end to all exploitive practices of doctors and psychiatrists who work
in the field of transvestism.

Street Transvestite Action Revolutionaries, *Manifesto* (New York, NY), flier, 1970.

5.Transvestites who live as members of the ppposite gender should be able to

&btain identification of the opposite gender.

6.Transvestites and gay street people and all oppressed people should have

free education, health care, clothing, food, transportation, and housing.

7.Transvestites and gay street people should be granted full and equal rights

on alllevels of society, and full voice in the struggle for liberation of all

oppressed people.

8.An end to exploitation and discrimination against transvestites within

the homosexual world.

9.We want a revolutionary peoples' government, where transvestites, street

people, women, homosexuals, blacks, puerto ricans, indians, and all oppressed

people are free, and not fucked over by this government who treat us like

the scum of the earth and kills us off like flies, one by one, and throws

us into jail to rot. This government who spends millions of dollars to go

to the moon, and lets the poor Americans strave to death.

POWER TO THE PEOPLE

S. T. A. R.

FIERCE! Info about LGBT youth FROM LGBT youth

My name is Erykah. I am 19 and I live in New York City. I am a Transgender female. Transgender means that I am a woman who was born biologically male and now live my life as a female. I work at the New Neutral Zone, a drop in center for lesbian, gay, bisexual and transgendered young people. In many ways, I am just like you. I go to work, I cook, I clean, I bleed. Last November, I left home. I was sad to leave my mom's house, but I was 18. I thought it was the right thing to do. I left by choice. I got to pack my stuff and take what I wanted. But that is much more than most of my peers. Everyday I talk to my mother, just like all my mother's daughters. These are things a lot of people take for granted, but to me they are blessings. Many young people are homeless because their parents didn't want gay kids around. Just like you don't want gay kids on your block. Your "efforts" to clean *your streets* is a big deal to me. Many of my friends are working the streets having to do what they have to do to survive. At my job, we call that "survival sex". It's hard to support yourself when you're young, homeless and queer. If you want these kids off your streets, please help us find them a place to go. If you put your energy into helping solve the problem of homelessness and homophobia/transphobia, everyone will win.

My name is Kristen. I am 22. I identify as Native American and African American. I am also transgendered. It is hard being transgendered, people don't want to help you. One day, I went into a neighborhood restaurant and they said to me "We don't serve your kind." They said I was prostituting. In actuality, I was trying to buy soup. Last week, I was arrested in the West Village while I was sitting on a stoop talking with a friend. Four cops arrested us. They never told us what we were being arrested for. They finally charged us with prostitution in court. I felt like I couldn't fight because I didn't have the money to pay for bail. They would have kept me in jail while my case made its way through court but I pled guilty just to get out of there. Now I have a police record. It's hard to be a person of color and queer in this neighborhood. I have lived in this neighborhood, where gay, lesbian, and transgendered people have lived safely in for a long time, where I paid rent to live. But I can't buy soup, or talk to my friends on the street there now. People always say "get a job, get a job." But it's not that easy. I have worked all kinds of jobs. I've waited tables, worked as a messenger, all sorts of things, but jobs aren't easy to find, and they are even harder to find when you are a lesbian, gay, bisexual or transgendered youth. But I can't tell my landlord that I don't have a job come back next month. Just like you are comfortable, I need to be comfortable too. What have you done to help lesbian, gay, bisexual, and transgendered young people? You don't want young people on your street, but I need a place to go. Going to jail won't help me. I need services.

FACTS YOU MAY NOT KNOW ABOUT LESBIAN, GAY, BISEXUAL, TRANSGENDERED AND HOMELESS YOUTH

- More than 90% of LGBT youth regularly hear homophobic remarks in their schools, and more than two-thirds experience verbal, sexual and physical harassment and assault.
- Among LGBT adolescents receiving services at a NYC agency for LGBT youth, 2 out of 5 have been physically assaulted, and more than 3/5's of this gay related violence had occurred in their homes.
  - *100% of LGBT youth in foster care have experienced homophobic verbal abuse in their group homes while 70% of these youth have experienced homophobic physical violence in their group homes*
- Over 35% of NYC's homeless youth are lesbian, gay or bisexual
  (This statistic does NOT include trans identified homeless youth)
- During Giuliani's term in office funding for youth has decreased
  1. *The Summer Youth Employment Program provided 40,000 youth with summer jobs in 1999 and only 15,000 in 2,000*
  2. *250 youth programs were closed*
  3. *$754,000,000 was taken from public education*

If you want more information please contact us at:

FIERCE! A project of the Ella Baker Center; 437 West 16th Street, Lower Level, New York, NY 10011 **Fax:** (646)336.6788 **Phone:** (646)336.6789 x.105 (Gabe) x.108 (Jesse) **E-Mail:** Thats_FIERCE@hotmail.com

FIERCE!, *Info about LGBT youth FROM LGBT youth* (New York, NY), poster, c. 2000-2001.

AgitArte (art by José 'Primo' Hernández), *Black Trans Lives Matter #say their names,* poster, 2020.

7 ~~SIX~~ BLACK WOMEN

Recently 6 young Black women have been murdered in Roxbury, Dorchester and the S. End. The entire Black community continues to mourn their cruel and brutal deaths. In the face of police indifference and media lies and despite our grief and anger, we have begun to organize ourselves in order to figure out ways to protect ourselves and our sisters, to make the streets safe for women.

We are writing this pamphlet because as Black feminist activists we think it is essential to understand the social and political causes behind these sisters' deaths. We also want to share information about safety measures every woman can take and list groups who are working on the issue of violence against women.

In the Black community the murders have often been talked about as solely racial or racist crimes. It's true that the police and media response has been typically racist. It's true that the victims were all Black and that Black people have always been targets of racist violence in this society, but they were also all women. Our sisters died because they were women just as surely as they died because they were Black. If the murders were only racial, young teen-age boys and older Black men might also have been the unfortunate victims. They might now be petrified to walk the streets as women have always been.

When we look at the statistics and hard facts about daily, socially acceptable violence against women, it's clear it's no "bizarre series of coincidences" that all six victims were female.* In the U.S.A. 1 out of 3 women will be raped in their lifetimes or 1/3 of all the women in this country; at least 1 woman is beaten by her husband or boyfriend every 18 seconds; 1 out of every 4 women experiences some form of sexual abuse before she reaches the age of 18 (child molesting, rape, incest) 75% of the time by someone they know and 38% of the time by a family member; 9 out of 10 women in a recent survey had received unwanted sexual advances and harassment at their jobs.** Another way to think about these figures is that while you have been reading this pamphlet a woman somewhere in this city, in this state, in this country has been beaten, raped and murdered.

*Boston Globe, April 1, 1979, p. 16.
**Statistics from the paper "Grass Roots Services for Battered Women: A Model for Long Term Change" by Lisa Leghorn. Available from the U. S. Commission on Civil Rights, Washington, D.C.

These statistics apply to all women: Black, white, Hispanic, Asian, Native American, old young, rich, poor and in between. We've got to understand that violence against us as women cuts across all racial, ethnic and class lines. This doesn't mean that violence against Third World women does not have a racial as well as sexual cause. Both our race and sex lead to violence against us.

One reason that attacks on women are so widespread is that to keep us down, to keep us oppressed we have to be made afraid. Violence makes us feel powerless and also like we're second best.

The society also constantly encourages the violence through the media: movies, pornography, Playboy, Players, Hustler, JET, record covers, advertisements and disco songs ("Fut Loves Chains Back On Me"). Boys and men get the message every day that it's all right even fun to hurt women. What has happened in Boston's Black community is a thread in the fabric of violence against women.

Another idea that has been put out in this crisis is that women should stay in the house until the murderer(s) are found. In other words Black women should be under house arrest. (Remember Daryal Margett, the fifth woman, was found dead in her own apartment.) If and when they catch the murderers we still won't be safe to leave our houses, because it has never been safe to be a woman alone

WHY DID THEY DIE?

in the street. Staying in the house punishes the innocent and protects the guilty. It also doesn't take into account real life, that we must go to work, get food, pick up the kids at school, do the wash, do errands and visit friends. Women should be able to walk outside whenever they please, with whoever they please and for whatever reason.

WE WILL ONLY HAVE THIS RIGHT WHEN WOMEN JOIN TOGETHER TO DEMAND OUR RIGHTS AS HUMAN BEINGS TO BE FREE OF PHYSICAL ABUSE, TO BE FREE OF FEAR.

The last idea we want to respond to is that it's men's job to protect women. At first glance this may seem to make sense, but look at the assumptions behind it. Needing to be protected assumes that we are weak, helpless and dependent, that we are victims who need men to protect us from other men. As women in this society we are definitely at risk as far as violence is concerned but WE HAVE TO LEARN TO PROTECT OURSELVES. There are many ways to do this: learning and following common sense safety measures, learning self-defense, setting up phone chains and neighborhood safehouses, joining and working in groups that are organizing against violence against women are all ways to do this.

The idea of men protecting us isn't very realistic because many of us don't have a man to depend upon for this—young girls, teen-agers, single women, separated and divorced women, lesbians, widowed women and elderly women. And even if we do have a man he cannot be our shadow 24 hours a day.

What men can do to "protect" us is to check out the ways in which they put down and intimidate women in the streets and at home, to stop being verbally and physically abusive to us and to tell men they know who mistreat women to stop it and stop it quick. Men who are committed to stopping violence against women should start seriously discussing this issue with other men and organizing in supportive ways.

We decided to write this pamphlet because of our outrage at what has happened to 6 Black women and to 100s and 1000s of women whose names we don't even know. As Black women who are feminists we are struggling against all racist, sexist, heterosexist and class oppression. We know that we have no hopes of ending this particular crisis and violence against women in our community until we identify all of its causes, including sexual oppression.

(Above) Combahee River Collective, *7 Black Women: Why Did They Die?* (Boston, MA), pamphlet, 1979.

The Black lesbian feminist collective Combahee River Collective published this pamphlet after a series of unsolved murders of Black women in the Boston area. The collective wrote that the murders, which police downplayed after claiming the victims were sex workers, needed to be understood as acts of both race- and sex-based violence.

(Left) New York Transgender Advocacy Group, *Protect Black Trans Women Rally* (New York, NY), flier, 2021.

(Top) Micah Bazant, Janetta Johnson, Danielle West and Transgender Gender-Variant Intersex Justice Project, *Police out of Pride*, pencil and watercolor, 2016.

(Bottom left) *#FreeThemAll*, button, n.d.

(Bottom right) Molly Crabapple, *#FreeBresha* (New York, NY), button, n.d.

Radix Media, *Justice for Freddie Grey / Disarm the Police* (New York, NY), poster, 2015.

FIGHTING FOR DEMILITARIZATION

Even though police departments like to project the public image of a beat cop walking the neighborhood, it has been 60 years since that was the primary way poor, working class, and communities of color have been monitored and regulated. Special Weapons and Tactics (SWAT) units were developed in the 1960s, in particular under the watch of the LAPD's Chief of Police Daryl Gates who claimed that, after the Watts uprising, police needed advanced, military-style tactics to respond to crowds. The units began receiving federal funding in the 1970s and exploded during the War on Drugs. The national turn to more conservative politics and "law-and-order" campaigning only increased after the Reagan years, with subsequent increases in militarization. With 1994's Violent Crime Control and Law Enforcement Act, and then 1997's 1033 Program, police forces expanded nationwide and local municipalities increased their police budgets and added hundreds of thousands of new cops. The continued prevalence of so-called "broken windows" policing (now long debunked as successful) and stop-and-frisk policies (eventually found illegal in New York City) increased both mass surveillance and the national prison population, which ballooned from around 400,000 in 1970 to over two million by the year 2000.

Since authorization of the 1033 Program, municipalities have been allowed to acquire military-grade weaponry including armored vehicles, aircraft, and sound cannons from the Defense Department

(Left) *Patrick Dorismond: 1 More Victim of Giuliani Time* (New York, NY), button, 2001.
(Right) *End Stop & Frisk* (New York, NY), button, n.d.

in order to perpetuate the failed War on Drugs. When protests erupted in Ferguson, MO in 2014 following the police killing of Michael Brown and later during the water protectors' encampment at Standing Rock in 2016, the spectacle of police using wartime tactics on protesters shocked many Americans. But tanks rolling through the streets at night were painfully familiar to those who had been working on the ground resisting police violence and to many Black, Indigenous, and immigrant communities who experience the police every day as an occupying presence. Today, most SWAT teams are deployed for drug raids, often without a warrant. It was a SWAT raid in 2020 that led to the death of Breonna Taylor.

Criticism of this militarization has been growing, and a portion of the national dialogue around defunding the police has been dedicated to exposing the level of militarization that has infected even the smallest of police forces. Groups like Dissenters, a youth-led anti-militarization organization, have been connecting US imperialism abroad to the militarized occupation of Puerto Rico, Indigenous communities across North America, and urban communities of color. They are leading the way in showing how the struggles against each of these must be connected.

(Left) Eian Dhruva, *Are We Feeling Secure Yet?* (Philadelphia, PA), poster, 2005.
(Right) Artist Unknown, *Homeland Security*, stenciled poster, 2000.

Fight Police Brutality!

We Demand:
Jail Killer Cops!
Stop in-custody beatings and harassment!
End police brutality!
End police corruption and drug dealing!
Elect community based police review broads!
Require community residency for all police!
End police immunity in off duty violations and crimes!
Zero Tolerance for Police Brutality!

The epidemic of police brutality targets youth, African Americans, Latinos, Native Americans, Asian Americans, Immigrants, the homeless, women and the Lesbian/Gay/Bi/Transgender people. To fight police abuse we must stand together under the banner, "An injury to one is an injury to all."

On Tuesday Oct 22, 1996 Wear Black!

Join us in the National Day of Protest to Stop Police Brutality Repression and the Criminalization of a Generation.

Rally at City Hall Park 1pm, March at 3pm
Take the N, R, 4, 5, 6 to City Hall

**Sponsored by: Oct 22nd Coalition Against Police Brutality -- NY
For Further Info: (212) 642-8812**

October 22 Coalition Against Police Brutality, *Fight Police Brutality!* (New York, NY), flier, 1996.

Rainbow / PUSH (People United to Save Humanity), *Busted! Youth & the Law in Illinois* (Chicago, IL), pamphlet, n.d.

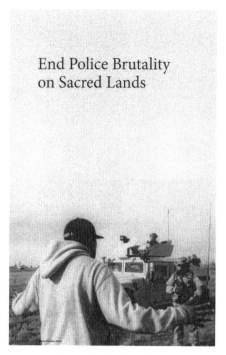

(Clockwise from top-left) *End Stop and Frisk / Silent March Against Racial Profiling* (New York, NY), flier, 2012.
Christopher Francisco, *End Police Brutality on Sacred Land* (Portland, OR: Eberhardt Press), poster.
Stop Mass Incarceration Network, *Ferguson is Everywhere*, poster, 2014.
Alec Dunn, *Domestic + Global*, from the *DE-MIL-I-TA-RISE* portfolio by Justseeds and Dissenters (Chicago, IL),
screenprint poster, 2020/21.

Revolutionary Action Movement (RAM), *Black America* (Detroit, MI), magazine, Fall 1964.

Black America was a literary journal created by the Revolutionary Action Movement (RAM). The journal published work by RAM members and Black nationalist thinkers like Muhammad Ahmad (known then as Max Stanford), James Boggs, and Harold Cruse as well as artists and poets associated with the Black Arts Movement. Poet and painter Askia Touré (who went by Rolland Snellings at the time) served on the editorial board.

CULTURAL ORGANIZING

Shortly after the assassination of Malcolm X in 1965, the poet Amiri Baraka (formerly LeRoi Jones) founded the Black Arts Repertory Theater (BART) with artist and activists Askia Touré (formerly Rolland Snellings) and Larry Neal. The Black Arts Movement, as Larry Neal would later write, was "the aesthetic and spiritual sister of the Black Power concept."[7] The poetry, jazz, and art that came out of this movement centered Black liberation and militant anti-imperialism, including resistance to police brutality. In 1985, reflecting on that time, Baraka wrote that the Black Arts Movement was meant to "fight for black people's liberation with as much intensity as Malcolm X our 'Fire Prophet' and the rest of the enraged masses who took to the streets in Birmingham after the four little girls had been murdered by the Klan and FBI, or the ones who were dancing in the street in Harlem, Watts, Newark, Detroit. We wanted an art that would actually reflect black life and its history and legacy of resistance and struggle!"[8]

The Black Arts Movement has been criticized for blatantly homophobic and anti-Semitic writing and for a swaggering machismo that centered Black men. However, some of its most enduring original members are Black and queer women. The poets Sonia Sanchez, June Jordan, Nikki Giovanni, and Audre Lorde all achieved mainstream success after the movement largely dematerialized. In her 1978 poem

---

7 Read more at "The Black Arts Movement," *Poetry Foundation*,
   https://www.poetryfoundation.org/collections/148936/an-introduction-to-the-black-arts-movement
8 Baraka, Amiri, "The Wailer," *Callaloo*, no. 23, 1985, p. 248–56.

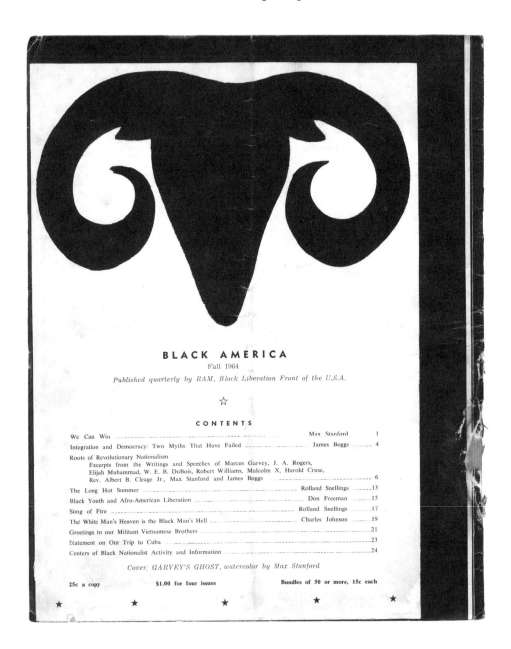

BLACK AMERICA
Fall 1964

Published quarterly by RAM, Black Liberation Front of the U.S.A.

☆

CONTENTS

Cover: GARVEY'S GHOST, watercolor by Max Stanford

25c a copy $1.00 for four issues   Bundles of 50 or more, 15c each

★   ★   ★   ★   ★

Various artists, *Hip Hop for Respect* 12" vinyl EP (US: Rawkus, 2000).

"Power," Audre Lorde wrote about the 1973 murder of 10-year-old Clifford Glover and the acquittal of the officer who shot him:

Today that 37-year-old white man with 13 years
of police forcing
has been set free
by 11 white men who said they were satisfied
justice had been done
and one black woman who said
"They convinced me" meaning
they had dragged her 4'10" black woman's frame
over the hot coals of four centuries of white male
approval
until she let go the first real power she ever had
and lined her own womb with cement
to make a graveyard for our children.

Decades later, the Black Arts Movement and the cultural nationalism advanced by the Black Panther Party would influence socially conscious hip-hop artists like Public Enemy, KRS-1, and other artists on Boogie Down Productions. These and other groups gained mainstream success with the rising antagonism to the police within youth culture. Public Enemy's "911 is a Joke" (1990) and N.W.A.'s "Fuck the Police" (1988) were both massively popular. Within the punk scene, hundreds of anti-police songs and records have circulated since the 1980s, from Doom's "Police Bastard" (1989) to the very name of the band Millions of Dead Cops. Films of that era, including Spike Lee's *Do the Right Thing* (1989), John Singleton's *Boyz N the Hood* (1991), and F. Gary Gray's *Set it Off* (1995) reflected the perspective of the politicized youth and the growing national awareness of police violence in Black neighborhoods. Lee's film was dedicated to the families of six Black people murdered by police or, in Griffith's case, a white mob: Eleanor Bumpurs, Michael Griffith, Arthur Miller Jr., Edmund Perry, Yvonne Smallwood, and Michael Stewart.

Public Enemy, *911 Is A Joke* 12" vinyl single (US: Def Jam, 1990).

MC Shan, *Time for Us To Defend Ourselves* 12" vinyl EP (US: Cold Chillin', 1990).

Dr. Joshua M. Myers, professor at Howard University and author of *We Are Worth Fighting For: A History of the Howard University Student Protest*, argues that:

Hip-hop was a major...in fact, influence is too small a word to really explain how important hip-hop was to [young activists'] consciousness. It was their language, it was how they made sense of the world, it was their philosophy of life. Black youth at the time knew perhaps better than most people what the effects of Ronald Reagan's economic policies were and so you find that their analysis ends up being reproduced in hip-hop music at the time.

The reason that that happens is because musicians were on college campuses engaging with students around these particular issues. I think study and knowledge is the fifth element of hip-hop for many people. When you see them all together, it's actually producing the possibility for Public Enemy's "Fight the Power," which is like the quintessential anthem, right? *That doesn't come out of the genius only of Chuck D, and only of [Professor] Griff and others. It's a collective movement that helps produce that particular moment.*

It's also not just the music that is explicitly political, it's also the LL Cool J's of the world, it's also the dance music. That's really important too, because it's showing how these black youth were living against the sort of creative destruction of their communities, that they were embodying resistance by creating joy and creating pleasure and creating the emotional release that hip-hop becomes.

And so to this day, they always remind me, that generation, Ras [Baraka] reminds me that we liked the ratchet stuff, too. And we still like the ratchet stuff. Because it's about the spirit; it's about our ability to live against other people's plans for us.

Dead Prez, *Police State* 12" vinyl single (US: Loud, 1998).

Paris (featuring Dead Prez & Public Enemy), *Freedom* 12" vinyl single (US: Guerrilla Funk, 2003).

Dr. Joshua M. Myers

Interviewed by BROOKE DARRAH SHUMAN

Joshua M. Myers is an Associate Professor of Africana Studies in the Department of Afro-American Studies at Howard University. He is the author of *We Are Worth Fighting For: A History of the Howard University Student Protest of 1989* (NYU Press, 2019) and *Cedric Robinson: The Time of the Black Radical Tradition* (Polity, 2021), as well as the editor of *A Gathering Together: Literary Journal.*

BROOKE DARRAH SHUMAN: Can you talk a little bit about your work? I'd also love to hear what differences you see between the young people, students and people in cities organizing in the 1980s and 90s versus what would have been the Black Panthers and the Young Lords in the 60s and 70s.

JOSHUA MYERS: The archives that I have and use for my book are actually private. They belong to two of the women who were organizers at Howard University who were students and members of Black Nia F.O.R.C.E. and were part of the effort to broaden Black Nia F.O.R.C.E. into a national organization in 1991. This is a period of time where you see increased organizing around police brutality in New York City. I'm going all the way back to Yusef Hawkins [murdered by a white mob in 1989], Eleanor Bumpurs [killed by police in 1984], and Michael Stewart [murdered by police in 1983]. Black Nia F.O.R.C.E. was comprised of people who were primarily from the New York City area. Even though they were Howard students, they're mostly from New York; there was a huge Philly contingent as well, New Jersey, some even from upstate New York. So they're shaped by that moment. They're also shaped by the idea that the police were an occupying force in Black neighborhoods in DC.

Howard University sat in a Black neighborhood in Northwest DC and it was heavily policed. At the same time, the police did not protect students who were at Howard and were actually antagonistic, in many cases, to the students at Howard. So there was not a separation the way you would expect, for instance, if it was Columbia University in the Harlem community, where the students are specifically protected, whatever that means (laughs), from whatever is happening in the broader community. Howard students clashed openly with the police. I mean literally clashed: fighting the police in the streets and surviving those fights, thankfully. It was almost as if the police were another gang that they had to worry about. Black Nia F.O.R.C.E. organized around police violence in DC and they also organized one of the major New York youth responses to the Rodney King verdict.

They were directly inspired by several organizations. First is really the Nation of Islam, who had a visible presence during the 80s and early 90s and had a huge impact in terms of disciplined response to the police and being protectors—not just protesters but protectors. The Nation of Islam did paramilitary training, and Black Nia F.O.R.C.E. did security for Public Enemy whenever Public Enemy performed.

BDS: Were they also influenced by the Black Panthers self-defense and Young Lords, or was it more Nation of Islam?

JM: It was really Nation of Islam first. The Nation of Islam has a paramilitary unit called the Fruit of Islam and that was the group that trained Black Nia F.O.R.C.E. in how to do this kind of work. In terms of the organizational structure, Black Nia F.O.R.C.E. were influenced by the Black Panther Party: they had an Executive Minister and the Minister of Internal Affairs and External Affairs, basically the same structure that you see with the Black Panther Party. When they became a national organization in '91, they adopted the 10 Point Platform and applied it to the 1990s. The direct influence of the Panthers was key, and generationally, they believed they had to finish the work of that previous generation. Ras Baraka was one of the founders of Black Nia F.O.R.C.E.; his father, Amiri, and his mother, Amina, were heavily involved in that work. Not necessarily with the Panthers, but certainly with that generation of activists. So this is literally the next generation.

When they founded the New Jersey chapter, Ras Baraka led a proposal to start the civilian review board in Newark in 1993 or 1994. At first it was an embrace of Black nationalist self-defense and self-determination, but also increasingly it became using leverage to win electoral races because that's part of the Black Power movement too.

BDS: So that wasn't seen as contradictory? The self-determination versus electoral politics?

JM: It wasn't. For them, it was a question of taking over the country (laughs). Especially in the cities that they were in, which were run by older people who were out of touch with what the young people saw as the issues. Ras Baraka was maybe 24 years old when he decided to first run for mayor. It was all about: "Let's take over and make the government actually be self-determining for Black people," which is a lofty ideal, but that's what they were after.

BDS: Can you talk about the music of that era and its influence on activists?

It was almost as if the police were another gang that they had to worry about.

JM: Hip-hop was the major, in fact, influence is too small a word to really explain how important hip-hop was to their consciousness. It was their language, it was how they made sense of the world. It was their philosophy of life. And it's also reciprocal in a very real sense because the hip-hop artists are getting things from them as much as they are getting things from hip-hop artists.

Many of the people who we all know as household names not only got their start at Howard but were actually influenced by what was happening at Howard among the student body at the time. So, when Public Enemy comes to Howard it's not because it's a special occasion but because they know that Howard is connected to what they're trying to do. Sister Souljah, when she comes out of Rutgers, builds a national organization based around Black youth, and Black youth at the time knew perhaps better than most people what the effects of Ronald Reagan's economic policies were.

Their analysis of neo-liberalism and state violence ends up being reproduced in hip-hop music at the time and the reason that that happens is because hip-hop artists were on these college campuses engaging with students around these issues. Most of these students are actually the first generation in their family to go to college, and so it's very class-oriented as well. Out of that momentum, Sister Souljah created what is called the Get Busy (General Education in Training Blacks United to Save our Youth) Tour. And that's where people like Chuck D, Kevin Powell, Doug E Fresh, Ras Baraka, and many others went around the country to talk about these political issues.

The other bridge figure is Haqq Islam. He was actually a member of the Five-Percent Nation. Many of these people who were in hip-hop activism were at the time. The mantra of Five-Percent Nation was "Do the Knowledge." Study and knowledge is like the fifth element of hip-hop for many people. Seeing this all together produces the possibility for Public Enemy's "Fight the Power," which is like the quintessential anthem, right? That doesn't come out of the genius only of Chuck D, and only of [Professor] Griff and others. It's a collective movement that helps produce that particular moment.

And it's not just the music that is explicitly political, it's also the LL Cool Js of the world; it's also the dance music that's really important, because it's showing how these Black youth were living against the creative destruction of their communities. They were embodying resistance by creating joy and creating pleasure and creating the emotional release that hip-hop becomes. To this day, that generation and Ras [Baraka] always reminds me that we liked the ratchet stuff too. And we still like the ratchet stuff. It's about the spirit; it's about our ability to live against other people's plans for us.

BDS: As we've been working on this project, it's remarkable to see how much backlash there is in history, every time there's any kind of progress. We're certainly seeing that right now in a really extreme way. I don't know if there was a national government response after the LA riots, or if there was some kind of tangible progress after that era. But I wonder if you can talk about either advancements or a backlash that activists saw.

JM: Oh, yeah. The backlash is increased gentrification, the backlash is surveillance. The backlash is the continuous neo-liberalization of life and the "tough on crime" laws that we see in the 1990s. It's all connected to the culture war. You see an immediate assault against hip-hop as led from the White House, in fact. Tipper Gore [creating the Parents Music Resource Center which pressured record companies to label music as violent or sexual]. Bill Clinton's so-called "Sister Souljah moment" is actually, I think, a direct condemnation of Black youth politics at the time.

I think one of the things that actually happens—and this is just my speculation, so keep that in mind—I think when you see hip-hop explode with things like "F the Police," and the quick backlash, and then all of a sudden, by the mid 90s, everybody is being more flashy and throwing their money around and wearing shiny suits. I think that was reinforced by politics that said, "Y'all can't talk about this stuff anymore." So, you get the era of hustler music with, ironically, Puff Daddy being one of the leaders, despite the fact that he was involved in Black Nia F.O.R.C.E. I think that could be linked to backlash politics, including the fact that Black people weren't in control of what music gets played.

BDS: What about progress from that era?

JM: There are people still resisting. Ras Baraka, he would say that the fact that he was able to eventually win the [mayoral] election was progress. It was a hard, long road and looks like probably a flash in the pan from the outside. Some would also point to the fact that many of the positions that were held by people outside of the Black community and quite frankly, outside the hip-hop community, with respect to the music in the early 90s, are now in Black hands. Many people that were in Black Nia F.O.R.C.E., for instance, are actually involved in the music industry as leaders, but these are also the Diddys of the world. And so do we exchange politics for ownership? I don't know. Maybe he did. Some would say that's progress. I don't know if that's progress or not.

Another thing I wanted to say is that education was an area where a lot of the generation saw potential. Many of them became teachers, in both independent schools and public schools. Today, I know at least two high school principals whose start was as a hip-hop activist. That's something that is lesser known as well: the role that that generation has in terms of being present in the public education system, both men and women.

But other than that, the police budgets are still inflated, so they didn't really make that much political progress. And there wasn't much conversation about abolition, at least, not on the East Coast. On the West Coast you can find those conversations, but there wasn't that much conversation on abolition. And Ras was interviewed in 2020 about abolition and he said, "I don't know about that." I think that's a reflection of the fact that that discourse wasn't part of their political maturity. It was out there but geographically it was mostly centered on the West Coast. I think now there's more of a national conversation but it's interesting because now that generation has been brought into the system. They don't necessarily see the connections between their own radical activism as youth and abolition today. That's something that I think is a political hurdle.

That generation also probably would not have been able to predict the co-optation of community policing and the way that it happened. One of the conversations that they were having in the 90s was that police need to come from our communities. They need to live in our city. Well, we know now that that doesn't actually transform anything about the nature of policing. One of their major beefs with the police was, "Y'all don't live here." Now we know that it doesn't matter where they live, because they actually have a function as police. I think many of them, today, hesitated around abolition, because of those other alternatives that they fought for like the civilian review board and community policing. I think it's a political hurdle to get over with Generation X. It's so funny, because they policed themselves in many ways, meaning they protected themselves, when it came to issues of people who committed acts of violence, right? They actually practiced transformational justice in their own spaces. As Public Enemy said, "911 is a Joke," so they actually had mechanisms in place if somebody committed violence against a member of their community.

There are also conversations among veteran political strategists today that Defund was a mistake. I spent almost all summer—it felt like all summer— arguing with older political activists around the question of Defund because there was a consistent belief that it was a messaging mistake. That dissipated a lot of the energy, especially after the election and now that this is not an urgent thing in the streets anymore.

But I do believe that among people who are already committed to abolition, it's an exciting time. We now have people writing about it, publishing about it, making it a part of the library. Now it's not just something that's on social media. Now you can be introduced to it in your sociology class. Ruth Wilson Gilmore is writing several books that are coming out soon. Mariame Kaba has two books now. Derecka Purnell. So in that sense, it's an exciting moment.

I think we have to uncover those stories of practices that didn't go by the name "abolition" that we were already doing this work, and we need to be able to connect the ways that we were already practicing alternatives to policing. Because if I go to the average Gen Xer and say, "abolition," they won't necessarily grasp what that means until I talk about their own personal and political experiences.

Critical Resistance, *Critical Resistance: Beyond the Prison Industrial Complex conference*, Illustration by Rupert Garcia, (Berkeley, CA), poster, 1998.

IMAGINING AN ABOLITIONIST FUTURE

The police might be the most visible arm of the carceral state, but the prison is always lurking in the background and incarceration remains part of the lives of hundreds of thousands of working-class people, BIPOC, and immigrants. Organizations that call for dismantling and demilitarizing the police naturally advocate for the end of prisons and a shift to non-violent, non-punitive rehabilitation options for those who commit acts of violence. In 1997, scholars Angela Davis, Ruth Wilson Gilmore, and Rose Braz co-founded Critical Resistance, an anti-incarceration and abolitionist organization. Critical Resistance used the term "abolition" to tie the current reality of mass incarceration to racialized forms of control from chattel slavery to convict leasing to Jim Crow laws in the South.

Critical Resistance popularized the concept of prison abolition by merging it with practical activism. In their pamphlet *What is Abolition?*, they lay out a simple argument for the end of both incarceration and policing in Black communities: "We cannot build strong communities when people are constantly being taken out of them."

Like abolitionist groups before them, Critical Resistance argued that reform of prisons was insufficient and only a total overhaul of the way that communities respond to harm will put an end to violence. They call for "a program of real economic development in both rural and urban areas, to make rural communities less dependent on prisons and urban dwellers less dependent on underground economies."

#ACAB, button, n.d.

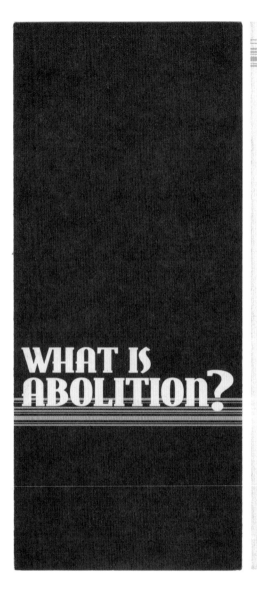

WHAT IS ABOLITION?

Critical Resistance's mission is to end the prison industrial complex (PIC). The PIC is a system that uses policing, courts, and imprisonment to "solve" problems. We don't agree that we need the PIC to keep us safe. Instead, we work to build safe and healthy communities that do not depend on prisons and punishment.

WHO WERE THE FIRST ABOLITIONISTS?

We take the name "abolitionist" purposefully from those who called for the abolition of slavery in the 1800's. Abolitionists believed that slavery could not be fixed or reformed. It needed to be abolished. As PIC abolitionists today, we also do not believe that reforms can make the PIC just or effective. Our goal is not to improve the system; it is to shrink the system into non-existence.

WHAT ABOUT PUBLIC SAFETY?

We all want safe communities. The question is how do we build safe communities? Is it by locking up and policing more and more people? Or is it by dealing with the causes of the harm that is called "crime" in our communities?

Even the worst kinds of harm do not happen without a reason. Putting people in cages does not solve any of the problems that lead to harm, like harmful drug use, poverty, violence, or mental illness. By separating people from their home communities, and isolating them in abusive and violent environments, these problems can even get worse. We take seriously the harms that happen between people. We believe that in order to reduce harm we must change the social and economic conditions in which those harms take place.

2011.002

Critical Resistance, *What is Abolition?* (Berkeley, CA), brochure, n.d.

For example, providing drug users with health care and harm reduction strategies instead of locking them in cages helps reduce the harm that drug use might cause. When public funding is directed into policing and prisons, budget cuts for social programs, including women's shelters, welfare and public housing are the side effect. These cutbacks leave women less able to escape violent relationships. Focusing more energy on creating safe and stable conditions instead of policing and imprisonment reduces harm.

Studies have shown that states with more prisons and prisoners do not have lower crime rates than other states. The PIC claims to be about safety and order. In reality, the PIC makes the lives of most people – especially the poor and people of color – less safe and more disordered. For example, poor people and people of color are often targeted by the cops based on the way they look. And even in instances where people call the cops to solve problems, the cops are often more disruptive than the original problem. We cannot build strong communities when people are constantly being taken out of them.

WHAT ARE THE ALTERNATIVES?

We do not have all the answers. But, we do know that people in other parts of the world rely on prisons and police far less than the U.S. does, and suffer from far less harm. We also know that communities where people have housing, food, education and jobs have the lowest crime rates. The best way to reduce harm is by building safe, healthy communities where people have their basic needs met.

WHAT CAN I DO TODAY?

Today, there are small steps that will move us toward abolition, such as:

* Instead of supporting construction of a new prison to make the horrible conditions that most prisoners live in a little better, we can push for alternatives that reduce the number of people locked in cages.

* Instead of calling the police everytime there is a conflict in our neighborhoods, we can establish community forums and mediation practices to deal with harm and conflict.

* We can build safer and healthy communities by working to eliminate barriers to housing and jobs faced by people coming home from prison to help them stay out of the system.

ABOLITION IS A REALISTIC VISION

The PIC did not always exist. The modern day prison is only about 200 years old. Even today there are places where people rely on each other instead of police, courts, and cages.

It has taken over 200 years to build up the PIC. We can't expect to take apart such a complicated system in a short time. The first slavery abolitionists began working decades before they won the abolition of slavery. Our struggle is a long one. Believing we can abolish the PIC is the first step.

Critical Resistance, *Slavery is Not Over Yet* (New York, NY), poster, 2001.

Contemporary groups like INCITE!, Project NIA, and Survived & Punished (the latter two founded by Mariame Kaba) have incorporated the legacy of Black feminism and queer activism into abolition work. These groups have pushed for the end of cash bail and harsh sentencing for both petty non-violent offenses and violent crimes, an end to the criminalization of youth in the school system, and the decriminalization of sex workers.

Mariame Kaba reflects on the reasons for starting Project NIA:

"I launched Project NIA in 2009...In Chicago at the time, I noticed a disconnect between policy and the direct community, and particularly the young people who I was in community with, who didn't really get to weigh in on the policies that were impacting their lives in such massive ways. Project NIA was an attempt to help support and create leadership pipelines for young people, particularly those who were impacted by the criminal punishment system, to have a voice in determining their own fates. Police violence was a huge part of that. They were always harassed, targeted, and violated by police."

As we imagine a different future, Mariame Kaba reminds us that

"We need to think about the lineages of these things in the long view. Our wins are not our wins alone; we are building off legacies, even of peoples' struggles and tactics that we didn't agree with."

Just as prison abolition movements have built on the work of previous slavery abolition, labor, and Civil Rights organizing, current movements to defund the police continue building on the work of prison abolitionists; these struggles are inextricably linked. In 2020, as the streets filled with protesters enraged by the police murders of George Floyd, Breonna Taylor, and Tony McDade, the Movement for Black Lives again took a defiant abolitionist stance: "We must reverse centuries of disinvestment in Black communities to invest in a future where we can all be connected, represented, and free." The demand to "Defund the Police" rang out across the country and energized the movement.

The uprising in the summer of 2020 was reported to be the single largest mobilization in United States history and led to a few important gains. In New York City, Communities United for Police Reform successfully campaigned to repeal the 50-A statute, which had shielded police disciplinary records from public scrutiny. The group had been organizing towards that goal for years, but were able to capitalize on the energy of the protests to make it happen. Some cities responded to the "Defund the Police" demand with cuts to police budgets and diverting funding to other violence-prevention measures like community mediator projects and social programs. Minneapolis, Milwaukee, Baltimore, Los Angeles, and New York City all saw either decreases in the budget or diversion of funds; almost $1 billion was cut from police budgets in total, thanks to unprecedented organizing success. Budget gains were as low as a 4% reduction in most cities, but Black feminist organizers like Black Visions Collective, Reclaim the Block

(Top) INCITE!, *Stop Police Brutality Against Women of Color & Trans People of Color* (New York, NY), poster. Illustration by Cristy Road.

(Bottom, left and right) *What's Racist Sexist and Just Plain Fucked Up About the NYPD?* (New York, NY), brochure, 2014.

Police violence is
systemic, racial, political, & unnecessary

The NYPD is not simply composed of corrupt or racist individuals. Racial bias is built into the whole architecture of policing and incarceration, and the justice system serves the political objective of oppressing non-white people. The militarized and overfunded police force occupies the streets of black and brown neighborhoods, harassing and abusing innocent people based on racist suspicion.

STRATEGIES OF VIOLENCE

The Baton **STREET HARASSMENT**

NYPD Stop and Frisk has been widely denounced as a form of racial profiling. But humiliating street harassment and illegal searches are well-established police practices that overwhelming target black and Latino people. The NYPD routinely conducts unlawful stops, searches, and seizures that they claim target "suspicious behavior." The same justification has allowed police officers to walk free after killing unarmed youths like Kimani Gray and Ramarley Graham.

The Gavel **SENTENCING**

Glaring inequalities in sentencing clearly demonstrate the racial bias of the law. Black and Latino people accused of drug crimes are significantly more likely to be sentenced to prison than white offenders. Despite national reform passed in 2010, sentences for possession of crack cocaine continues to drastically outweigh sentences for powdered cocaine.

The Shackles **INCARCERATION**

The U.S. prison population has exploded in the past three decades due to increased policing and longer sentencing mandated by the nationwide War on Drugs. One in every fifty Americans is under a form of correctional supervision. Many prisons are overcrowded, and state governments are increasingly contracting private companies to run prisons.

RACIAL AND POLITICAL CONTROL ARE TWO SIDES OF THE SAME COIN

Liberation movements, especially Black, Latino, and labor struggles, share a history of police repression. The NYPD and other police forces continue to break up strikes, evict families from their homes, beat down nonviolent protesters, and harass the poor and working communities. Today, mass outrage and political pressure to end police violence have challenged the unlawful and inhuman killings of innocent youth of color by police. But the most powerful police strategies of racial and political control remain uncontested.

The U.S. has about **5%** of the world's population.

The U.S. has about **25%** of the world's prisoners.

DAILY POLICE REPRESSION TARGETS COMMUNITIES OF COLOR

Stop and frisk is just the tip of the iceberg. Police pretend to have unlimited authority to search people of color in their own neighborhoods. Because cops need to fill quotas, they routinely write up ridiculous charges, embellish or exaggerate situations, and fabricate crimes entirely. When their illegal searches do not bear fruit, too many officers will either plant drugs or accuse the "suspect" of resisting.

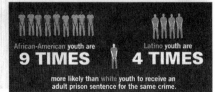

African-American youth are **9 TIMES** | Latino youth are **4 TIMES**

more likely than white youth to receive an adult prison sentence for the same crime.

in Minneapolis, and many others see impact beyond budget numbers and recognize this as a step towards the larger abolitionist project to divest from violent policing and fund safe Black communities.

Jawanza Williams, member of the Free Black Radicals and VOCAL-NY and organizer of Occupy City Hall 2020 reflects on the Defund movement and abolition:

We knew that [Occupy City Hall] had to be a space that centered Black, queer, feminist politics, modalities and frameworks because that's how I understand abolition and how to get there. So, those had to be the fundamental values of the space. We also said that the space is not a particular organization, but there is a particular demand. There can be other demands, but the primary demand is that we want to defund the NYPD by at least a billion dollars and fund housing, education, social services, and care.

[The Defund movement] has been watered down to a phrase—an inflammatory phrase— and labeled as bad messaging. And there are those people who try to say: Defund means community investment. I'm like, it is community investment, but it also does mean reducing the scope, the power and influence of NYPD towards abolition, and we need to not be afraid of saying that.

In the year that followed, police officials and the Patrolmen's Benevolent Association led a campaign to label the Movement for Black Lives as extremist and anti-public safety and to falsely claim that crime was increasing because of anti-police reforms. Studies conducted by criminologists and criminal justice non-profits have shown time and

again that increases in police budgets do not decrease crime and similarly, defunding their budgets does not increase violent crime, but the press, both right-wing and mainstream, continue to amplify unsubstantiated police talking points.

Minneapolis failed to pass the city charter amendment that would have replaced the Minneapolis police force with a Department of Public Safety informed by abolitionist practice, but 44% of residents voted in favor of the ballot question, showing that the movement in Minneapolis had reached many residents and that those residents thought reforms were insufficient. New York City elected former NYPD officer Eric Adams as mayor in 2021; he was quick to enact policing practices not used since the Giuliani era. Six City Council members elected on a Defund platform voted against Mayor Adams's 2023 budget when it failed to divest from the NYPD budget to reinvest in community programs.

Abolitionist visions for public safety may remain nascent but are still insurgent in much of the United States. There is no easy win, but this project reminds us that we are not alone. The legacy we build on is strong, and the tools at our disposal are many.

mpd150, *Enough is Enough: a 150 year performance review of the Minneapolis police department: Expanded Edition* (Minneapolis, MN: self-published), 2020.

Anonymous, *George Floyd* (Brooklyn, NY), painting reproduced as sticker, 2020.

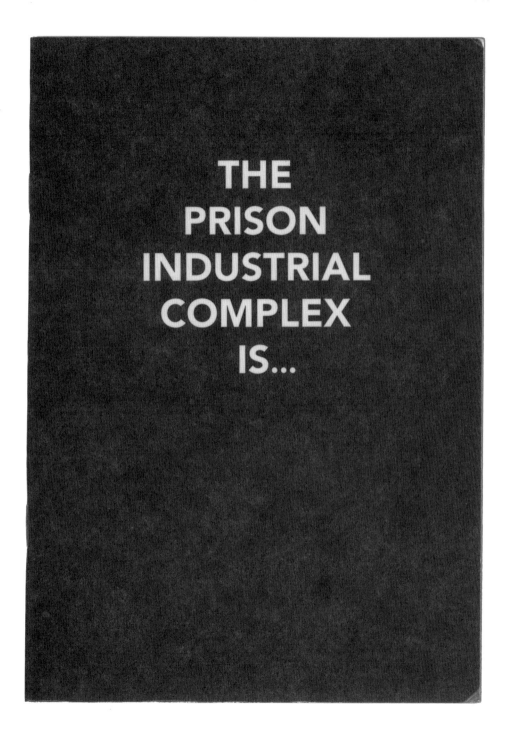

Pages 141-143: Project NIA, *The Prison Industrial Complex is...* (Chicago, IL: self-published), 2011. Illustrations by Billy Dee.

Project NIA, *The Prison Industrial Complex Is...* (Chicago, IL: self-published), 2011. Illustrations by Billy Dee.

The Prison Industrial Complex
takes a foothold in your
underfunded public school when
counselors are replaced with cops.

(Top) VOCAL-NY (design: Max Wittert), *Join the Movement to Defund the NYPD, Occupy City Hall*, social media graphic, 2020.

(Bottom) NYC-Democratic Socialists of America Racial Justice Working Group Defund the NYPD (design: Tracey Fu), *Refund the People*, social media graphic, 2020.

Artist Unknown, *Don't Shoot!* (Brooklyn), hand painted sign, 2020.

(Top) Lane Sell and Jason Das, *End Police Impunity* (Brooklyn, NY), poster, 2020.
(Bottom) Lane Sell, *Disarm NYPD NOW* (Brooklyn, NY), poster, 2020.

Josh MacPhee, *Defend / Defund* (Brooklyn, NY), 2-sided placards, 2020.

Occupy City Hall / Abolition Park 2020

During the summer uprising of 2020, and after months in lockdown for COVID-19, organizers in New York City staged an occupation of City Hall Park that lasted nearly a month in downtown Manhattan. Initially, the occupation was formed to pressure the City Council to pass a budget that would partially divest from the NYPD. Different groups had different demands; the Free Black Radicals, VOCAL-NY, and Communities United for Police Reform proposed $1 billion worth of cuts from the NYPD's $5.6 billion and DSA-NYC's #DefundNYPD campaign demanded half the budget and half the staff. The encampment had teach-ins every day and night, including ones about health care, housing, education, abolitionist thought and living unhoused. There was a library, art, music, set-ups for three meals a day and water, toiletries, NARCAN and other resources. After the initial week-long occupation, the Council voted on the 2021 budget on a video conference meeting that members of the occupation projected onto a screen while hundreds sat in the street and watched. The Council passed a budget after midnight on July 1st that redirected half a billion of the NYPD budget to school officers and other so-called safety resources, which most, if not all, at the encampment found insufficient. A hiring freeze of incoming officers remained in effect until October 2020; meanwhile, most of the city's workforce, including teachers, sanitation workers and healthcare workers, remained in a hiring freeze for the following year. The official Occupy City Hall ended, but continued in the same space as Abolition Park for another three weeks until the NYPD violently swept the camp in the early morning of July 22, 2020.

Beginning of the Occupy City Hall encampment, June 24, 2020. Credit: VOCAL-NY

Interviews with:*

- **JAWANZA WILLIAMS,** Free Black Radicals and Voices of Community Activists & Leaders (VOCAL-NY)

- **BIANCA CUNNINGHAM,** Free Black Radicals

- **CHERYL RIVERA,** Democratic Socialists of America Racial Justice Working Group & Abolition Action

Interference Archive: Where were you in the summer of 2020? Were you in New York City for COVID?

JAWANZA: I think I have to go back a little bit further before the summer starts. In March 2020, we all knew that COVID was starting to spread around the world but New York City wasn't shut down yet. And at VOCAL-NY, where I work, we suddenly had to pivot and begin to respond to COVID-19 while the city left out any meaningful consideration for people experiencing homelessness. The city kept saying: everybody stay home and to us we were like, what do you mean, stay home? There's a homelessness crisis! We were fighting for the city to convert vacant hotel units so that people could get out of congregate settings, which we all knew were driving COVID-19 infections and ultimately deaths.

And then in May 2020, George Floyd was murdered. For me, I don't only think about George Floyd, I think about Breonna Taylor and I also think about Ahmaud Arbery. I was devastated and I was thinking: this shit is still happening to Black people, even in 2020. I was thinking about not just my own immediate mortality, but also about the mortality of the tens of thousands of people dying from COVID-19. I'm an anti-capitalist, and to me so much of how we were responding or really not responding to COVID-19 had everything to do with markets and everything to do with the maintenance of neoliberal, hyper-conservative, white-supremacist ideological frameworks. The right-wing capitalist framework did not want to be disrupted, and it was going to cost people their lives.

Note: These interviews were conducted separately with Interference Archive in 2022.

BIANCA: When the pandemic started, I was in a job where I was doing national organizing and so I went from traveling 90% of my time to all of a sudden being at home, quarantined like everyone else. I probably stayed in my house and didn't leave from March 2020 until May. The first time I came out of my house, besides to go to the grocery store, was when George Floyd was murdered. I remember being so overwhelmed. I was watching sources like Unicorn Riot all week and seeing the people in Minnesota just popping off. I was sobbing every single night feeling like, "What the hell is going on outside right now?" And then by the end of the week, I was out there right in front of the Barclays Center with thousands of other people getting pepper sprayed by the police. I had forgotten how to breathe, if that makes sense. I'd forgotten what it felt like to be in a big crowd and now all of a sudden, here I am with my mask on in the thick of this action, getting pepper sprayed.

CHERYL: I had been doing mutual aid since the beginning of the pandemic, Abolition Action had mobilized very quickly and we ended up jumping into the mutual aid effort week one of the pandemic. So I was already in a bit of crisis mode. But the mutual aid felt very—it felt like we were filling in the gaps of what had been abandoned by the state.

And then in May, the George Floyd protests started. I kind of go back and forth on what word to use. We often would say: the uprising. And I think that we said it more when we felt hopeful. And now, often, I hear more people say "the 2020 protest," which feels like a smaller word and I think makes it smaller than it actually was. Because it was the biggest protests ever in US history. And it was incredible, the way it felt. There were all these different contingents. You had your mommies and daddies of Park Slope, who would like to be woke and would come out for the 3pm march and they'd be inside by 6pm. They knew they could be there for the march that wasn't going to get too rowdy. And then there was the after dark contingent when everyone knew once it started getting dark the police were gonna start beating your ass. Little skateboard kids. I have a lot of respect for what I call the skateboard boys of New York, who come out in these wild droves of rage. Good for them.

IA: When things sort of erupted in this way, I know that there had been many Black Lives Matter protests in New York before this, but there was something really unique about that summer. And I'm wondering how you felt and what your experience was like?

CHERYL: It really felt different than other protests I'd been in before. I've been in Fuck the Police protests against the transit cops and Black Lives Matter protests, but I had never experienced that level of holding the city hostage in the best way possible. This was impossible to ignore. I hadn't felt the power of a crowd in that way before. But I also hadn't felt the vacuum of left leadership in this country. It's crazy how little political analysis there is about why we are here, what this moment is about and what we can do.

JAWANZA: I don't know if you know this writer Arundhati Roy, she wrote *The God of Small Things* and *The Ministry of Utmost Happiness*. She's an Indian leftist and political thinker. And in March or April of 2020, she wrote an article about COVID-19 and she posited that COVID-19 was perhaps a portal. We're being asked and given an opportunity collectively: do we want to drag the carcass of our old world: capitalism, racism, the caste systems, the pollution, etc, into this new world? We're being told we got to pause and because the whole world had to pause, that's unparalleled. That's never happened ever before in human history in the way that it did. So it was an opportunity unlike any other and I think that's sort of what led to Occupy City Hall being possible. I felt that in my heart: we were being given an opportunity for the rapid advancement of our collective consciousness.

I was feeling a lot of devastation. Some of us fought very hard for Bernie Sanders, not because of the personality of Bernie Sanders, but because of the platform that Bernie had, like Medicare for All. But everybody rejected him. And then it became so clear how important everyone's equitable, comprehensive access to health care was because of this pandemic. I was feeling a lot of nihilism, but I've heard that in order to be a good Marxist, you have to remain hopeful. The occupation at City Hall was built on the hope that people would respond, because there was no guarantee, ultimately, of change. I'm still shocked that it happened.

IA: Shocked, because?

> **JAWANZA:** Well, shocked because more people took direct action that summer, across the country, than ever before in American history. This is a fact. My question is: where are the organizations that are able to absorb those people, so that we can activate them more intentionally? There were so many people across the country and across the city of New York alone doing marches, direct actions. There was all this energy—transformative energy, the stuff of revolution—and it just so desperately needed a focus.

IA: How did the occupation of City Hall happen?

> **JAWANZA:** There was a formation called Free Black Radicals of Black organizers who were interested in abolition, ultimately. At the same time, the Communities United for Police Reform had begun to develop collective demands—we wanted to see at least a $1 billion reduction in NYPD and reinvestment in housing, health care, education, social services.

> **BIANCA:** I was a part of the Free Black Radicals, which is a direct action group of Black folks who made the decision to drop all of their titles within their organizations and whatever else that we used to cling so tightly to really be in deep solidarity with one another around trying to defund the police and also just create some larger movement within our city around issues of police brutality and racial justice. It's funny because, before we came together, many of us didn't see each other as allies; our organizations are white-led and were often in conflict about things. But we really quickly realized that we were all we got. Our organizations didn't care as deeply about this issue and we just had to come together as, first and foremost, Black folks to do this work. Nobody else was going to do it.

> By late June, we started to see two things happen. Number one: the momentum started to slow down in terms of people in the streets. And the second thing was that a lot of those actions and protests were being co-opted by the political machine. It was actually demobilizing to have people who have marched around all day in the heat for a month, you know, to see no end results. And so Jawanza at VOCAL-NY came to us and asked, how can we respond? We felt like people were really focused on this macro level

of white supremacy and racism, not even knowing that in our own backyard, decisions were about to be made that would impact people where we live.

JAWANZA: Because I'm so used to running issue-based campaigns, I was thinking, like: who are the people that can actually give you what you want? And I remember thinking to myself: Why is no one marching to City Hall? Why is no one saying to [Speaker of the New York City Council] Corey Johnson, Mayor de Blasio, we want you to defund the NYPD by this amount, and then demonstrate that demand by getting hundreds or thousands of people into the park? We didn't want the mayor or any councilmember to say, look, everybody's talking about "defund the police," but there's no one who is asking us to do that. We needed them to see that there were ten thousand people outside that wanted to see that happen.

BIANCA: VOCAL-NY came to the Free Black Radical space and said, "Hey, y'all, we're gonna call for this action. We have no idea what's gonna happen. We don't want to own it. We just want to have people come here to a certain place and then see what happens." We all committed to supporting this very vague (laughs), undefined thing. But of course, VOCAL are our brothers and sisters and siblings in the movement and we were all for that. So they called the action and we just watched it grow.

Housing justice teach-in with Housing Justice for All organizer. Occupy City Hall / Abolition Park 2020 credit: Brooke Darrah Shuman

IA: Why did you or your group feel it was important to occupy this space and have it be a physical encampment?

> **BIANCA:** We were looking for escalating actions. A lot of what we saw prior to that were nice rallies and marches around the neighborhood. After Floyd's murder, there was all this righteous anger and frustration. Groups were setting things on fire and really in direct conflict with police. And then we saw it go from this very hands-on, direct approach to people deciding: we're just gonna march for peace. I think that made us feel like we needed something deeper, more rooted in community, and something that had an analysis. We thought an occupation would be something that would turn up the heat and put pressure on the city.

IA: What were the demands for the occupation?

> **BIANCA:** We wanted to defund the police by, we were saying a billion dollars, but really $3 billion is what we wanted. We wanted money to be reallocated to restorative justice officers and restorative justice programs that would train people up to have those skills within their school sites. That was our real demand: more mental health education and funding for social services. One of the byproducts of creating this space that was well resourced and had food and had Wi-Fi was that, you know, probably 60% of the people that were sleeping over were without a house. It just really illuminated the need for services.

> **JAWANZA:** One of the things that I feel like I always want to correct the record on is, look, we never said *only* a billion dollars, we said *at least* a billion dollars, and a lot of people had problems with us not just saying straight out: "We need to abolish the NYPD." And I was always like, yes, of course I want to abolish the NYPD as well, but we are assessing our power. We're assessing the moment. We know we're not going to be able to abolish the NYPD this week. I mean, maybe we should have believed more, though, who knows?

> **CHERYL:** There were a few of us from the Democratic Socialists of America (DSA)'s Racial Justice Working Group at the City Hall encampment that were doing #DefundNYPD and abolition teach-ins. VOCAL-NY and a few

of the other main organizers of the City Hall encampment made a demand of $1 billion. And we were like, immediately, let's make our demand half the budget, half the force. It's catchy, it's nice. It's maximalist. Because we already knew that the City was not going to give us what we asked for so we thought, ask for more. By doing a maximalist demand, we're thinking, let's force their hand and let's let the public know that the NYPD spent $6 billion, because most people don't know that.

Occupy City Hall / Abolition Park 2020 credit: Brooke Darrah Shuman

IA: Can you talk about the space itself and the teach-ins?

BIANCA: The first night, it was nothing, right? I think maybe we had 200 people sleeping in the park. We ordered food for people and we just had it on the ground. The next day, a restaurateur came to us and said, "I have all these resources to help you all out. I have a refrigerator." Within hours, she just showed up and was setting it all up and said, "Let me handle food." One by one, organizations and people with resources would just come in and be like, "Hey, we're gonna set up the people's library over here. Is that cool?" And then all of a sudden we had all these things for people to build structures and sleep in. That's when a large houseless population ended up coming because we had Wi-Fi and three meals a day. We were getting donations from all over the world. I actually started the Instagram page the first night and by the morning, I was trying to coordinate food donations and other donations from everywhere into the space.

I couldn't believe how many people were like, "Okay, well, we need some sort of programming." We started to reach out to some housing rights organizations, youth employment organizers, and had them build a schedule. It was a beautiful space. One night, on one side of the park, I remember the DSA was doing a Defund the Police training, and there were like 300 people at that. And then in another space, Jews for Racial and Economic Justice were having Shabbat and holding a prayer service for Black Lives Matter. It was just really vibrant.

CHERYL: Our teach-in was based on our #DefundNYPD zine and my other group Abolition Action did a history of policing and prisons. We laid this timeline out on the ground at the encampment and allowed people to contribute their personal experiences or facts that they knew related to policing and prisons. So it became a collaborative exercise. The vibe there was just really great. People were present and really wanting to participate and do something together. It was possible to have 100-plus people in person sitting on the ground and really listening with focus.

IA: What were the guiding principles of the encampment? What were your goals for the space itself?

JAWANZA: I know, for people from the Free Black Radicals, we felt that the space, number one, had to be a space that centered Black, queer, feminist politics because that's how I understand abolition and how to get there. And we knew it needed to be a safe space, where everybody was welcome, including the people that might already live in the park overnight. So we had to be intentional about: do we have food? Are we going to have things to offer people? Are we going to be willing to connect people to direct services? What about people that use drugs? We had to make sure that we had on-site Naloxone kits and people who knew how to do patrols for people that might need help.

And we had, you know, we got people to donate money to it. There was a laundry service. There was a people's library, there was a People's Bodega, everything free of charge. There were three hot, good meals a day distributed to hundreds and thousands of people some days. All of that was through mutual aid networks. I think that mutual aid is a beautiful concept and that it's something we will always be doing as communities. But we also are not letting the government off the hook. I refuse to be like: we don't need the government, let's just do some mutual aid. No, no, no. Welfare is mutual aid on a scale that we need.

Watching the budget vote, June 30, 2020 credit: Jabari Brisport

I think that action gave us an opportunity to really think about what it is that we're talking about when we're talking about Black Lives Matter. It's not just that police maim, shoot, kill, injure Black people, but this is also about: how do we radically transform the conditions of people's experience? How do we change the experience of violence, poverty, gun violence? We should be ending homelessness, we should have comprehensive mental health care services. I think Occupy City Hall was a model of what it looks like when people try to take that love, care and compassion into their own hands. And it's also a reminder of the limits of mutual aid projects that don't have the backing of billions of dollars to meet the immediate and wide ranging needs of many people.

There were some rocky periods where we were trying to maintain safety in the camp without police. The action was not organization-specific so that meant that any activist was welcome and could set an agenda. And some people wanted to directly confront the police. I'm personally not interested

I think Occupy City Hall was a model of what it looks like when people try to take that love, care and compassion into their own hands.

in trying to go toe-to-toe with a paramilitary force because we will not win, we will never win. We have to instead lean on the egalitarian values of a democratic society. That's my worldview because I'm also having to account for people that are vulnerable.

IA: Can you talk about the night of the budget vote?

CHERYL: Yeah, the fake budget. It didn't have anything that people wanted. The City Council and the mayor and the media framed it as a $1 billion cut. No one at the encampment bought it. Everyone was like: Fuck, this is bad. De Blasio was saying "I'm gonna move that money into the budget for the Department of Education (DOE)," but the budget was still for school safety officers. So we're like, that's not cutting the police budget force, that's merely MOVING carceral forces to the DOE!

BIANCA: We were angry. The Free Black Radicals had had a press conference the day before and that was one of our very first times stepping out as a visible collective. As Black activists, we called out the Black establishment [City Councilmembers] Laurie Cumbo and Adrienne Adams: the people who were claiming to be with us. They were saying "Black Lives Matter," right? Now, these are Black leaders that we want to support, Black women that we don't want to attack, but we had no choice. Our main target was Speaker Cory Johnson, but we also had to call out some of the other more established Democrats on the Council and that included Black folks. It was really hard for us to do that, but we were really angry and we wanted to make them uncomfortable.

On the other hand, the night of the budget vote was really beautiful. We realized that people in the space felt like we weren't doing enough; they thought the occupation itself was not an action. And so we asked, how can we direct energy towards something that would be useful to accomplishing this budget goal? We did direct action training and took crews of folks in the night shift to go in front of Speaker Cory Johnson's house and other residences, to do wake-up actions. We had people deploying on the hour to locations that we thought were going to be strategic to hopefully make somebody really uncomfortable and let them know that we're watching them making their decisions. We also had a huge screen where we streamed the vote. You would have thought it was the NBA finals or the Super Bowl the way that everybody was crowded around, cheering and booing every council member as they made their remarks and put in their vote. Through that process, we were able to educate folks. It was a really beautiful thing to see people being so engaged. In the end, the city actually added $330 million dollars to the budget. They turned it into a labor issue. The City Council said: if we do what you are asking, this would mean firing all of these Black women who hold positions as officers in schools, and so they actually allocated more money to them and said that they were supporting Black women.

IA: What do you think was won that summer?

BIANCA: I believe we were able to radicalize a whole group of people who hadn't been active prior to this, and get them to really commit to this type of organizing. A lot of people I spoke to said this was their first protest and occupation. I also think we won an argument about mutual aid as organizing. Even the organization I was a part of at the time didn't really believe in mutual aid, they didn't think of it as organizing and they didn't think it had a place in the movement. The work we did proves that they were wrong. Mutual aid is fundamental to community organizing. I also think that reverberations of the work have continued. We trained, in a matter of a couple of weeks, seven thousand people across the country on abolition and defund movements based on what was happening in our own city that they could then use in theirs. That is a win.

CHERYL: In 2020, there were a lot of council seats up for reelection so we thought this was a good opportunity. DSA was already putting together this slate of candidates called "DSA for the City." There were six City Council people who ran and we created the Defund pledge and got them all to sign it. It was a public safety pledge basically saying, this is our vision for our communities: defund the NYPD and refund communities. Our line was, the city budget is a reflection of our priorities, it's a reflection of what we care about. And right now, it says we care a lot about cops, but it doesn't say we care about housing or about schools. Our DSA for the City slate was of course on board, but then we also tried to get signatures from other council members. Unfortunately, of our slate, I think only two out of six won. So it wasn't a great sweep for us. But we did get a lot of signatories outside of

DSA to sign. Currently, in the City Council, we have 17 people who have signed this pledge, which is, you know, not the majority, but it's a good minority block to have in City Council.

After that we started doing tabling and canvassing in all five boroughs. Recently, we started doing these community conversations in housing projects with local state senators and city councilmembers. Having representatives there often gives credibility for the average person but we're also just trying to help start a conversation with people around what public safety means to them.

IA: **And how do those conversations go? What do you think is one of the challenges for having a conversation about abolition with someone that is maybe new to that?**

CHERYL: The challenge is always that people say: "Abolition is not realistic." But they don't have to be abolitionists to be aligned with this Defund campaign. I think it's super important for us to never back down from our abolitionist vision. But we don't have to ask them to be abolitionists immediately. What we're asking is: do you believe that we need to invest more in our communities? People immediately ask: "What will we do when we don't have cops?" Which is certainly a topic that we've talked about in our Political Education group, but not necessarily the topic we need to talk about with the average person. Instead we start with: What does safety look like to you? What are the things that you would like to see the city spend its money on? It's usually not cops. Usually, it's: I have rats. My rent is high. There are no activities for the kids. People say that all the time. There's no programs for kids.

IA: **It's crazy how quickly the cops were able to politically organize and retaliate. I wanted to know if you had thoughts about the backlash as you see it in New York?**

BIANCA: Yeah, it was completely demoralizing to go from having lots of support, not only worldwide but around the city, to then electing a cop for mayor. We really realized, again, that it's all about identity and that identity politics is not going to go away. It's also really hard to position yourself as opposed to the

Black establishment, especially when so many of us have to work so closely with folks inside the political establishment to "get things done."

JAWANZA: I was very frustrated for a lot of 2021 because most people are so terrified of the phrase "Defund the police" now. All the Democrats have pushed it away from them. Even organizations that claim to be leftist have pushed it away. Just because a phrase is not palatable, or a demand is not palatable does not mean that we recoil and don't use it. If our communities don't understand it, we've got to teach them. There are Black Democrats who are centrists or right-wing, if you ask me, suggesting that Black communities don't want to defund the police, and I'm like, well, they don't want to defund

Occupy City Hall / Abolition Park 2020 credit: Brooke Darrah Shuman

the police whenever you frame it the way you're framing it, but if they *understood* what we're talking about, then I think that they would agree with us. So trying to reach them, that's a different task for a community-based organization.

CHERYL: The backlash happened because the cops are organized, but also because these various groups and institutions have an interest in keeping things as they are. *The New York Times* and the media, for instance, consistently ran stories about how Defund across the United States was leading to increases in crime, which was just not true. I wasn't surprised that the backlash started immediately, but I guess I am a little shocked at how many people believe we actually did defund the police. Because...does it look like we defunded the police? If you just look around? Have they been defunded? You know what looks defunded to me? The trashman. There's no garbage pickup. But people really bought it.

IA: And just to finish up, can you talk about what abolition means to you?

JAWANZA: I think it was really—how do I say this, [Occupy City Hall] was, it was one of the most beautiful, and most disturbing things I have ever participated in, and it was everything I needed to remind me that what we're calling for, this different kind of future, abolition, is possible. It just reminded me of all of the work that we have to do to engage in principled struggle, and how to respond to violence without police. I think we have our work cut out for us, but if anything, what that demonstration taught me was that it is possible for us to do things radically different.

BIANCA: Abolition to me means a space of birthing something new. It's shedding and unlearning all of the old ways of domination and violence and our way of being together and coming together out of mutual respect but also of mutual benefit.

There were a lot of conversations that popped up at Abolition Park about what safety means and I think that the movements that came out of the occupation are trying to define safety in their neighborhoods right now. The conversations that we had have transitioned away from defund the police to: what does safety look like for you? Because we feel like that's the actual place to start.

LEARN MORE

No More Police, Mariame Kaba and Andrea J. Ritchie, The New Press 2022

We Do This 'Til We Free Us, Mariame Kaba, Haymarket Books 2021

Becoming Abolitionists, Derecka Purnell, Astra House 2021

Set the Night on Fire: L.A. in the Sixties, Jon Wiener and Mike Davis, Verso Books 2020

Fight the Power: African Americans and the Long History of Police Brutality in New York City, Clarence Taylor, New York University Press 2018

The End of Policing, Alex S. Vitale, Verso Books 2017

Fear City: New York's Fiscal Crisis and the Rise of Austerity Politics, Kim Phillips-Fein, Metropolitan Books 2017

Captive Genders: Trans Embodiment and the Prison Industrial Complex, Eric A. Stanley and Nat Smith, AK Press 2011

Can't Stop, Won't Stop: A History of the Hip-Hop Generation, Jeff Chang, Picador/St. Martin's Press 2005

Are Prisons Obsolete?, Angela Davis, Seven Stories Press 2003

"Policing in America," *Throughline*, NPR, April 8, 2021

Every individual murdered by police leaves behind a family and a community; these families and communities often become the nexus of incredible and important organizing work. We encourage you to look for these groups in your own local community, learn their stories, and connect with their work.

Interference Archive imagines the possibility of a radically different future. As a physical archive of social movement history, its shelves contain the treasured, salvaged, dynamic notions of that existence—elucidating the histories of movements past while stirring the imaginations of today's organizers, educators, students, and everyday people seeking to discover their role in shaping a better future.

Interference Archive is a Brooklyn-based, volunteer-run community space and public archive, home to tens of thousands of individual cultural works created through and for the power of social movements. We are rooted in the belief that our shared histories should be held in common and accessible to all. Our mission is to encourage critical and creative engagement with the histories of people mobilizing for social transformation by exploring the relationship between cultural production and social movements through an archival collection, public exhibitions, a social center, talks, screenings, publications, workshops, and a rich online presence.

Interferencearchive.org / info@interferencearchive.org

Partner & Partners is a worker-owned design practice in New York focusing on web, print, and identity work with clients and collaborators in archives, local government, art, and activism. We prioritize projects and groups that promote social, economic, and environmental justice, with actionable visions for a just future.

partnerandpartners.com / info@partnerandpartners.com

ABOUT COMMON NOTIONS

Common Notions is a publishing house and programming platform that fosters new formulations of living autonomy. We aim to circulate timely reflections, clear critiques, and inspiring strategies that amplify movements for social justice.

Our publications trace a constellation of critical and visionary meditations on the organization of freedom. By any media necessary, we seek to nourish the imagination and generalize common notions about the creation of other worlds beyond state and capital. Inspired by various traditions of autonomism and liberation—in the US and internationally, historical and emerging from contemporary movements—our publications provide resources for a collective reading of struggles past, present, and to come.

Common Notions regularly collaborates with editorial houses, political collectives, militant authors, and visionary designers around the world. Our political and aesthetic interventions are dreamt and realized in collaboration with Antumbra Designs.

commonnotions.org / info@commonnotions.org

BECOME A COMMON NOTIONS MONTHLY SUSTAINER

These are decisive times ripe with challenges and possibility, heartache, and beautiful inspiration. More than ever, we need timely reflections, clear critiques, and inspiring strategies that can help movements for social justice grow and transform society.

Help us amplify those words, deeds, and dreams that our liberation movements, and our worlds, so urgently need.

Movements are sustained by people like you, whose fugitive words, deeds, and dreams bend against the world of domination and exploitation.

For collective imagination, dedicated practices of love and study, and organized acts of freedom.

By any media necessary.
With your love and support.

Monthly sustainer subscriptions start at $15.

commonnotions.org/sustain

Graphic Liberation:
Image Making and Political Movements
Josh MacPhee

978-1-942173-87-8
$20.00
192 pages

What is the role of image and aesthetic in revolution? Through a series of interviews with some of the most accomplished designers, Josh MacPhee charts the importance of revolutionary aesthetics from the struggle for abolition by Black Panthers, the agitation during the AIDS crisis from ACT-UP, the fight against apartheid in South Africa and Palestine, as well as everyday organizing against nuclear power, for housing, and international solidarity in Germany, Japan, China, and beyond.

In twelve interviews, political designer and street artist Josh MacPhee talks to decorated graphic designers such as Avram Finkelstein, Emory Douglas, and more, focussing on each of their contributions to the field of political graphics, their relationships to social movements and political organizing, the history of political image making, and issues arising from reproduction and copyright.

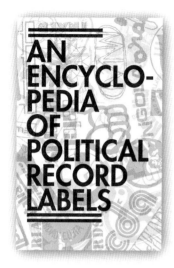

An Encyclopedia of Political Record Labels
Josh MacPhee

978-1-942173-11-3
$24.95
208 pages

An Encyclopedia of Political Record Labels is a compendium of information about political music and radical cultural production. Focusing on vinyl records and the labels that released them, this groundbreaking book traces the parallel rise of social movements in the second half of the twentieth century and the vinyl record as the dominant form of music distribution.

Just as the Civil Rights Movement leaps onto mainstream headlines in the early 1960s, the 33rpm "Long Player" and 45rpm single invade people's stereos. All the major Civil Rights organizations release vinyl records of speeches, movement songs, and field recordings—setting the pace for the intertwining of social movements and easily distributed sound recordings. This relationship continues through the end of the twentieth century, which marked both the end of apartheid in South Africa and the dominance of the vinyl format.

From A-Disc (the record label of the Swedish Labor Movement) to Zulu Records (the label of free jazz pioneer Phil Choran), *An Encyclopedia of Political Record Labels* is a compelling panorama of political sound and action, including over 750 record labels that produced political music. Each entry features the logo of the label, a brief synopsis of its history, and additional interesting information. Truly international in scope, over two dozen countries and territories are represented, as well as a myriad of musical styles and forms.

The Printed Legacy of the U.S. Radical Left, 1970–1979
Edited by Brad Duncan and the Interference Archive

978-1-942173-06-9
$27.95
256 pages

Finally Got the News uncovers the hidden legacy of the radical Left of the 1970s, a decade when vibrant social movements challenged racism, imperialism, patriarchy and capitalism itself. It combines written contributions from movement participants with original printed materials—from pamphlets to posters, flyers to newspapers—to tell this politically rich and little-known story.

The dawn of the 1970s saw an absolute explosion of interest in revolutionary ideas and activism. Young people radicalized by the antiwar movement became anti-imperialists, veterans of the Civil Rights and Black Power movements increasingly identified with communism and Pan-Africanism, and women were organizing for autonomy and liberation. While these movements may have different roots, there was also an incredible overlapping and intermingling of activists and ideologies.

These diverse movements used printed materials as organizing tools in every political activity, creating a sprawling and remarkable array of printing styles, techniques, and formats. Through the lens of printed materials we can see the real nuts and bolts of revolutionary organizing in an era when thousands of young revolutionaries were attempting to put their beliefs into practice in workplaces and neighborhoods across the U.S.

How We Stay Free:
Notes on a Black Uprising
Edited by Christopher R. Rogers, Fajr Muhammad, and the
Paul Robeson House & Museum

978-1-942173-50-2
$18.00
208 pages

In the midst of a global pandemic and a nationwide uprising sparked by the murder of George Floyd, Philadelphians took to the streets establishing mutual aid campaigns, jail support networks, bail funds, and housing encampments for their community; removed the statue of Frank Rizzo— the former mayor and face of racist policing; called for the release of all political prisoners including Mumia Abu-Jamal; and protested, marched, and agitated in all corners of the city.

How We Stay Free collects and presents reflections and testimonies, prose and poetry from those on the frontlines to take stock of where the movement started, where it stands, and where we go from here. A celebration of the organizing that sustained the uprising, *How We Stay Free* is a powerful collection that invites us all to celebrate Black life, find our place in an ongoing rebellion, and organize our communities for the creation of new, better, and freer worlds.

Making Abolitionist Worlds:
Proposals for a World on Fire
Abolition Collective

978-1-942173-17-5
$20.00
272 pages

Making Abolitionist Worlds gathers key insights and interventions from today's international abolitionist movement to pose the question: what does an abolitionist world look like? The Abolition Collective investigates the core challenges to social justice and the liberatory potential of social movements today from a range of personal, political, and analytical points of view, underscoring the urgency of an abolitionist politics that places prisons at the center of its critique and actions.

In addition to centering and amplifying the continual struggles of incarcerated people who are actively working to transform prisons from the inside, *Making Abolitionist Worlds* animates the idea of abolitionist democracy and demands a radical re-imagining of the meaning and practice of democracy. Abolition Collective brings us to an Israeli prison for a Palestinian feminist reflection on incarceration within settler colonialism; to antipolice protest movements in Hong Kong and elsewhere; to the growing culture of "aggrieved whiteness," to the punitive landscapes of political prisoners to the mass deportations and detentions along the U.S. southern border. *Making Abolitionist Worlds* shows us that the paths forged today for a world in formation are rooted in antiracism, decolonization, anticapitalism, abolitionist feminism, and queer liberation.